TRAINING YOUR MIND FOR SPLIT-SECOND DECISIONS

GEOFFREY MOUNT VARNER, MD, MPH

CONTENTS

Acknowledgments vii
Preface xi
Introduction xiii

1. Leadership 1
2. Human Physiology and Psychology 6
3. Decision Fatigue 10
4. Split-Second Decisions and the TLC Framework 15
5. Mindset Needed for Split-Second Decisions 32
   Practical Application: 41
6. Preparing for Split-Second Decisions 42

PREPARING FOR SPLIT-SECOND DECISIONS
   1. Reading 53
   2. People 59
   3. Blind Spots 61
   4. Meditation 65
   5. Exercise 67

7. Six Key Steps to Split Second Decisions 69
8. Split-Second Decisions – An Extra Dose 93
9. Prepare To Battle Your Demon – The War 108
   Conclusion 112

References 117

TRAINING YOUR MIND FOR SPLIT-SECOND DECISIONS

This book is a work of nonfiction. The information and advice contained in this book are based upon the research, and the personal and professional experiences of the author.

Copyright © 2020 by Geoffrey Mount Varner

All rights reserved. No part of this publication may be reproduced, scanned, uploaded, stored in a retrieval system, or transmitted, in any form or by any means, electronic, mechanical, photocopying, recording, or otherwise, without the prior written permission of the publisher.

Print ISBN: 978-1-7342566-6-6

ACKNOWLEDGMENTS

Special thank you to my family, my wife Angela, Brooke, Geoffrey, Coca Cola, Trinity Health, Harvard University, Hampton University, Dr. Battle, Larry Warren, Dr. Ed Bessman, Traffic, Sales and Profit, MSN, Forbes, Dr. Linda Arnell Mount, Sean Wintz, Honorable Daneeka Cotton, Dr. Mulagha, Honorable Donnaka Lewis, Stephanie, Dr. Reggie Eadie, Mel Spruill, Jon, Joyce and John Muscats, Dr. Robert Giles, Dr. Terri Jodrie, Buchanan Family, Jailynn, Jesse, Joey, Jaide, American College of Emergency Physicians, Centers for Disease Control, CDC, Genesis II class, Braydon, Landon, Camden, Washington DC Fire and EMS, Joe, Anton, Apple Inc, Tisa Giles, American Psychiatric Association, Lamar and Ronnie, Alpha Phi Alpha Fraternity Incorporated, Freddie and Krystal, Delta Sigma Theta, Coach P, Dr. Clark, Mike, Alpha Kappa Alpha, University of Maryland Undergraduate, Connie Wintz, Dr. Pines, Omega Psi Phi, Keyon and Jennifer, Bowie State, Dr. Breaux, Jaleah, Kappa Alpha Psi, Kimberly Parks, Jay, Gary Brown and family, Phi Beta Sigma, Marquette, Kemlia, Iota Phi Theta, Angela Alsobrooks, Dr. Thorton, Sha Cannono, Alfred Street Baptist, Ryan, Sigma Gamma Rho, Dr. Shane, Brittany, Deangelo, Lauren Brooks, Wrens, Kirk Weems, ESADC Fire and EMS, Clothidia, and the list goes on.

TRAINING YOUR MIND FOR SPLIT-SECOND DECISIONS

GEOFFREY MOUNT VARNER, MD, MPH

PREFACE

This time it was different. I was deployed with the Maryland National Guard as a physician as part of the 2005 Hurricane Katrina relief efforts in Louisiana. I was there days before the massive relief. Meaning, I witnessed horrific devastation. This was around the time that I began to really look at leadership and decision-making.

Then there was H1N1, also known as the Swine Flu, in 2009 that killed 12,469 people worldwide. I was the chief and chair of a large academic emergency department that had to prepare and respond to the H1N1 pandemic. The leadership lessons learned, as a result, were life-changing. During this time, I started to build the framework for developing *Split-Second Decisions* but I was still missing pieces to the puzzle.

As the SARS-COVID-19 crisis began to unravel further, I witnessed that it was unlike any virus our medical leaders had dealt with or seen in the past. The SARS virus wreaked unimaginable devastation and depredation. In an effort to aid with the relief, I elected to go to the front lines to treat patients. I was front and center with the enemy.

In that very moment, it was the *Split-Second Decisions* that were being made, that caused substantial death and destruction. In

Preface

comparison, the casualties by most models could have been less. However, this crisis led to the nation's citizens needing to suddenly become leaders and executives within their own households and required them to make critical and rapid decisions. Throughout the COVID-19 pandemic, families, organizations, and churches were making life and death *split-second decisions*.

At the peak fall out of the pandemic, I asked myself, "as a nation, are we properly prepared and trained in making *split-second decisions*?" And if not, would we continue to just guess and throw the wrong puzzle pieces at the situation as faulty solutions? As we have seen in so many crises before, those who are prepared fare better. With the 2019-2020 pandemic looming over our heads at a magnitude such as this, it is more important than ever to realize the need for focused and intense split-*second decision* training in nearly every aspect of our lives. For more information go to splitseconddecisions.com

INTRODUCTION

"Ma'am, we're considering charging you with manslaughter for killing your child."

One cold winter night, Mary noticed that her six-week-old daughter, Sarah, was fussier than usual. Sarah had not eaten dinner, so Mary took her temperature. The baby had a fever. Her breathing was also different. She contemplated taking Sarah to the hospital, but because of the harsh weather, she decided to wait until morning. Meantime, to keep a close eye on her child, Mary decided to let Sarah sleep beside her. Mary's decisions, all of them made within split-seconds, resulted in a devastating domino effect.

In the ER that morning, my colleagues and I received a call from paramedics stating that they had an unresponsive six-week-old female in full cardiac arrest and that they would be pulling into the ER in a matter of minutes. Although, the paramedics had appropriately initiated the Advanced Pediatric Life Support Protocol before arriving, Sarah unfortunately could still not be saved. She was pronounced dead at 4:15 a.m. that day.

The ER staff is required to inform the police of all pediatric deaths. Several detectives interviewed Sarah's mother, Mary, who understandably in her devastation and shock, was speechless. As I walked past the room, I listened to one of the detectives inform Mary that they were considering charging her with manslaughter. Her neglect was criminal enough to have possibly contributed to the death of her child. As you can probably imagine, this was an unimaginable scene, on many levels.

Suppose you are a parent who has just lost a child and to make matters worse, you are now being told it's your fault. What runs through your mind? How do you explain what is happening to your spouse, your parents, your circle of colleagues and friends, or even your other children? There is no real acceptable answer.

Suppose, on the other hand, you had received training to make *split-second decisions*, during let's say, a prenatal CPR workshop. The outcome for anyone in such a situation as Mary, would in all likelihood, been very different.

According to an article in *Psychology Today*, "How Many Decisions We Make Each Day," by Dr. Eva Krockow, discusses how in a single day, we make about 35,000 decisions. Of these, many experts suggest that roughly 70 of those decisions are life-changing or life-impacting and that most of those decisions are *split-second decisions*. Now, that is a lot of decision-making!

In the example above, it was not just Mary who had to make a split-second decision about her baby that night. She began a chain of responses, of course. Still, the first responders' decisions had an impact, as did the police detectives who interviewed Mary after her child died. There were many *split-second decisions* in a very short time, all of which involved baby Sarah.

I am an emergency medicine physician, a father, and a decision expert. Every time I go to work, I witness the positive and negative impacts of the decisions that have been made on life and death and the rippling effects those decisions have on the loved ones of the deceased, the doctors who tried to save them, and on the pre-hospital providers and the ER staff as well. ER doctors must think and respond with great urgency, synthesizing information, and making countless decisions that are often *split-second decisions,* a great number of which people's lives depend on.

Introduction

Now let's take a moment to rewind, to my pre-COVID days when I worked as the Medical Director for the Washington, D.C. area. During that time, I was in charge of all the acute care delivery and transports for an area that contained over four million people. And if there was a protest, rally, major diplomat in town, or severe weather event, the demand and expectation of emergency services increased. In fact, at times, we had to open a central command center to monitor events throughout the city. I remember receiving sudden calls about mass casualties or situations that threatened the fabric and safety of our nation's emergency healthcare delivery system, the Emergency Medical Services. In this capacity, it was my responsibility to make *split-second decisions* under time constraints, often with limited information. And just as often, the outcome of my decisions had severe consequences. Regardless, I had to make split-second decisions, and no matter the outcome, be prepared to make the next decision. We will discuss this further later in the book.

The elephant in the room. I know that you are wondering, "What is this ER doctor going to teach me about making split-second decisions? My decisions do not involve life or death." While your *split-second decision* may not likely lead to the immediate loss of life, one wrong, *split-second decision* could lead to the death of your business, loss of jobs, loss of contracts, loss of employees, hiring the wrong employees, and the list goes on. Hence, *split-second decisions* impact every aspect of our business lives. Later, you will see, *split-second decisions* impact our personal lives as well.

As a result of over 30 years of decision-making research, in tandem with my experience as an ER physician, a city executive, and a private company executive, I have developed a unique, but intentionally, simple method for making *split-second decisions*. It is useful in many areas and disciplines. My life has been shaped, trained, and centered around developing *split-second decision* skills. I have trained thousands to master these invaluable strategies. I have trained first responders, teachers, parents, executives, athletes, CEOs, leaders, pilots, and many others, to implement my techniques in to their daily lives. Essentially, the method I have developed can be used by anyone who must make decisions that impact people's everyday lives, directly or indirectly.

What follows is a description of what is known as the TLC framework for *split-second decisions*. This framework is about to change how you will go about making decisions. It will explain the three main components that constitute a *split-second decision*—time, lack of information, and consequences—and the best ways to use them for epic results.

1

LEADERSHIP

OWN IT

A patient overdosed on a dangerous substance, and I had to order charcoal for the patient to help neutralize the substance and thus make it less lethal. Yes, I mean charcoal, the thick, black, gritty substance. The patient was very drowsy and not completely cooperative. I ordered a nasogastric tube, also known as an NG tube, which is a large plastic tube that is placed down the patient's nose that goes directly to the stomach, commonly used in the emergency department. This would allow us to deposit charcoal into the tube, and to go directly in to the patient's stomach, where we needed the charcoal to be.

The nurse who had only been an ER nurse for about six months placed the NG tube and noticed that the patient was coughing after the tube was placed. She made the split-second decision to administer the charcoal down the tube but abruptly stopped because the patient started violently coughing and clinically started to experience acute distress. The nurse called for help, and I immediately assumed command of the situation. In the end, I had to place the patient on a ventilator. I admitted the patient to the ICU for a long and complicated recovery.

When placing an NG tube, coughing is a sign that the tube may have gone down the wrong orifice and may have not been appropriately placed. As it turns out, the nurse had placed the tube incorrectly. Instead of the tube terminating in the patient's stomach, where it was supposed to end, the tube was mistakenly inserted into the patient's right lung. Due to the tube being directed in to the patient's lung, the charcoal that the nurse administered went there as well. Charcoal is toxic to the lungs and therefore this caused the patient to immediately begin experiencing severe and complicated difficulty while breathing.

While I may not have administered the charcoal or been in charge of making sure the nurse had been appropriately trained on the placing and assessment of an NG tube, I was the captain of the ship. It was my patient, and I had to own the error. As the captain, it was my responsibility to make sure that everyone was trained to make split-second decisions.

There are thousands of books written about leadership. They teach you how to manage people, money, budgets, etc. The books often motivate you to be a better leader to those around you. I have found those books incredibly helpful and inspirational.

One day, it would be great if someone would take the best chapter or section from each book and combine them and make a mega book about leadership. In the meantime, split-second decisions is a book that includes mega experiences from many industries and lives.

The split-second decisions method is about more than just leadership. It is about what kind of person you are now, what kind of person you want to become, what kind of leader you want to be, and what kind of person you need to be during a crisis. Unless trained, during a crisis, we revert to our most primitive and most dominant emotions. If you have handled crisis through the lens of fear in the past, then you will likely manage your next crisis through the lens of fear. If you fumbled through your last split-second decision through the vibration of anger, then your next split-second decision will be anger. Also, if you get an adrenaline surge as you address split-second decisions, then you will likely experience the same surge in your next split-second decision. For the record, many who experience a "rush" during a crisis or split-second decision are prone to making snap decisions when a snap decision is not needed.

Again, we revert to our most primitive decision-making mechanisms during a crisis and split-second decisions. Using the newest scientific research, simplest techniques, and the TLC framework, we are going to move you massively forward at managing your emotions during split-second decisions and a crisis. We are going to make you a star, the go-to person. Most importantly, we are going to help you prepare for your next split-second decision.

Most of our decisions are emotionally steeped. Merely being self-aware of the active dominant emotions at that time and knowing how it impacts your decisions minimizes the uncontrollable aspects of the emotions they likely impact. It is important to control the controllable variables and minimize any negative impact of uncontrollable variables.

There are over 27 different emotions. The most common emotions that impact our decisions and especially our split-second decisions are the following:

1. Fear
2. Sadness
3. Fatigue/Tiredness
4. Happiness/Joy
5. Helplessness
6. Anger

We will briefly review and discuss the acute impact of these six emotions in a later chapter.

Principle: Own It

You must accept that you own it. Yes, as the leader, you own everything. If a bad decision is made because you did not have enough information from those below you, then it is your fault for not teaching them what and when they needed to share with you. If your superiors do not give you the resources or flexibility that you need to maximize your decisions, then you did not adequately communicate your needs before the situation arrived. It is a hard pill to swallow, but once you do, it is motivating.

This is true for leaders of families, clubs, churches, and so on. If those you lead are not functioning at the level they need to perform when you need them to, it is because you did not prepare them appropriately. This is true for all of us. It has been through my own experiences, successes, and failures, that I have come to understand this principle. If you own it all, it opens your mind to all possibilities. Accepting ownership frees your mind. After all, you do not have to worry about who to blame. There is no one to blame, but you. The possibility of failure is viewed differently when you own the assignment.

Failure could be as simple as you not preparing your team for what you know could or is going to happen. For instance, in one particular patient situation, my not owning everything led to the loss of someone's life. I was the physician team leader of two cardiac medical arrests that arrived at the emergency department at the same time. I was the only physician available, so I managed both codes. There was one ER tech who was working on both the codes with me. He not only mixed up a few orders but gave me the wrong laboratory results. There was a specific medicine that should have been given, which would have more than likely saved the patient's life, but because of the results, it was not given.

As the ER physician executive, I should have made sure that everyone was appropriately trained. I should have made sure that everyone on the team knew what to do. Yes, I could blame human resources, the ER educational coordinator, the chief technologist, or even the nurse manager or trauma director. But, as the physician leader, it was incumbent on me to be sure that everyone was appropriately trained for the situation that I knew was coming – a medical resuscitation. I was the sole owner and was the one to blame; I had to own everything in the resuscitation bay. No excuses.

Again, I know this is a hard pill to swallow, but if leadership were easy, then everyone would lead. If you own it, then you can fix it. You do not have to wait for an analysis report; you can put whatever needs to be in place now to ensure you accomplish your goals. You must own everything in the sphere of your control. You are the cavalry. Make sure that you show up and lead!

Practical Application:

I could have been upset with the nurse or perhaps the nursing manager. I knew that it was a new nurse as well. I knew that you had to pay special attention to new graduates in any area of medicine. I had to own the fact that it was a complete failure of my leadership. I should have been hypervigilant and led a training session on how to make split-second decisions that would have captured an exponential number of decisions. It would have played a major role in preventing this accident.

Owning it means that the only person to blame is you. It grows you as a leader. Ownership unleashes restricted forces that would have inhibited you from impacting or making decisions in areas that were not officially considered yours. But because you own everything, every area that impacts your ownership is yours. Nothing is restricting your thinking.

2

HUMAN PHYSIOLOGY AND PSYCHOLOGY

HOW PHYSIOLOGICAL RESPONSES TO STRESS CAN INTERFERE WITH DECISION-MAKING

A wide range of stressful experiences can influence human decision-making in complex ways beyond the simple predictions of a fight-or-flight model. Many important decisions are made under stress. For example, stock traders must make financial decisions under time and psychological pressures. CEOs make quick decisions during the Board of Directors meetings. First responders make life and death decisions while simultaneously dealing with the ubiquitous, common difficulties that life offers us. This includes family concerns, safety concerns, and complicated interpersonal relationships, etc.

In this section, we will discuss how your body responds to stress while making decisions. While there are millions of physiologic factors involved, we will focus on four areas:

- Endocrine system (the hormones)
- Central nervous system (brain and psychology)
- Cardiovascular system (heart and heart rate)
- Genetics (inheritability)

Lastly, we will look at some of the ways by which you can train your brain to cope with the stressful responses in ways that are more effective.

First, we must understand some of the basic terms and definitions, namely stress and cognition. Typically, stress is described as either one of two main types, acute stress or chronic stress.

- Acute stress is a transient state of arousal with the distinctive apparent onset and offset patterns.
- Chronic stress is a continuous state of arousal in which an individual's perceived demands are more significant than the inner and outer resources available for dealing with them. Stated less technically, stress comes from the needs of our past and expected pressures of our future.
- Whereas, cognition is the ability of our brain to process the acquired knowledge and understanding through thought, experience, and the senses.

Stress often originates in an area of the brain known as the hypothalamus-pituitary-adrenal-axis (HPA), a series of interactions between endocrine glands in the brain and the kidney, mutually linked by positive-and-negative-feedback pathways. They control your body's reaction to stress. Substances involved in these systems, such as catecholamine, corticosteroids, and cytokines, have to facilitate and inhibit influences on the central nervous system related to cognitive and emotional processes, underlying decision-making. When your brain detects a stressful situation, your HPA axis explicitly releases a hormone called cortisol, which primes your body for instant action. Presumably, the cortisol elevation may allow for the preparation of cognitive resources of reengagement toward an anticipated situation. Therefore, when optimal arousal levels and attention systems are established, higher-order cognitive mechanisms can proceed.

Nevertheless, high levels of cortisol over a long period wreak havoc on your brain. Chronic stress increases the activity level, and several neural connections in the amygdala, your brain's fear center, and as the levels of cortisol rise, electric signals in your hippocampus, the part of your brain associated with learning, memories, and stress, starts to deteriorate. Chronic or constant surges in cortisol may cause your brain to shrink in size over time. Too much of it results in loss of synaptic connections between neurons and the shrinking of your prefrontal cortex, the part of your brain that regulates activities including concentration, decision-making, judgment, and social interactions. Additionally, these changes set the stage for more serious mental problems, like depression and eventually, Alzheimer's disease.

The cardiovascular system, along with the endocrine system, plays a role as well. There is often an increase in heart rate during acute stress response as a result of elevated adrenalin levels. The increased levels also improve performance and the ability of rapid cognition, while larger increases in heart rate during stress impairs your ability to make optimal decisions. We will discuss this later in the book.

From a psychological perspective, stress impacts our decision-making by disturbing our standard thinking pattern and capacity. When we have less thinking capacity, we have less available resources for evaluating choices and options. Therefore, our decision-making is reduced in its effectiveness. There are many ways in which this occurs.

One way is that we become myopic in our thinking. Meaning we are less imaginative and have lack foresight or intellectual insight. We end up narrowly focused on the information related to the problem and tend to neglect other data. Another way that stress affects decision-making is that it leads people to make a decision more quickly than they usually do. People in high stressful situations often rely on their intuition largely. We know now that intuition is based on past experiences and is much more subjective to error and bias than conscious thought. For example, once you are stressed, if you are put in an environment that you know well and given a simple test, you will likely respond fine. However, if you are placed in a completely novel environment and given the same easy questions, you will likely not perform as well.

Additionally, the effects of stress may filter right down to your brain's DNA. An experiment showed that the amount of nurturing a mother provides to it's newborn pups has an essential role in determining how those babies will respond to stress later in life.

The pups of nurturing moms tended to be less sensitive to stress, because their brains developed more cortisol receptors, which stick to cortisol and dampen the stress response. The pups of neglected moms had the opposite outcome. Some did not manage stress as well as the pups who had been nurtured.

These are considered epigenetic changes, meaning that they affect which genes are expressed without directly changing the genetic code. However, there is a surprising result that the epigenetic changes caused by one single mother rat were passed down too many generations of rats after her. In other words, the results of these actions were inheritable (NYU Langone Medical Center, 2014).

We are living now in a time when we can measure and manipulate many factors that we could not in the past, and the science of stress is an unsurprisingly rich field of investigation now. There are several ways we can reduce the impact of stress on decision-making:

- The most potent weapons are exercise and meditation.
- Improving the quality, not the number of people in your life who impact your decisions.
- Having secure social networks has been shown to reduce stress levels. Talking to family, friends, and colleagues who we can share problems with.
- Learn to control your breathing. This involves deep breathing and being aware and focused on your surroundings. These activities combined decrease your stress and increase the size of the hippocampus, thereby improving your memory.

3

DECISION FATIGUE

"I did not realize how tired we were"

The parents called 911 to have their child, let's name him Robert, taken to the emergency department for evaluation by an emergency physician for flu-like symptoms. On this particular night, there were torrential rains with flooded streets everywhere, so it was challenging and time-consuming for paramedic crews to respond to calls.

The paramedics protocols require providers to assess the patient and then transport the patient to the closest appropriate hospital. Meaning, if the patient has a heart attack, the provider is expected to take the patient to the nearest hospital that has a cardiac team even if that means bypassing other hospitals. A good example would be if you are at work and your colleague slips and falls, stabbing themselves with a pen that lodges in their eye. The most common reaction would be to take the patient to the closest ER. But if the ambulance were called, the paramedics would take the patient to the nearest trauma center, even if that means passing the nearest hospitals. One final example, if the paramedics have a pediatric patient with an acute life-threatening injury, they're going to transport the patient to the closest pediatric hospital even if that means bypassing several closer hospitals.

Back to the story, the paramedic team arrived at the patient's home to awaiting and ready to go parents. The crew evaluated the child and assessed a few mild respiratory issues. Reportedly, the child did not "look too bad." So, the team decided to tell the patient's parents to monitor him and to make sure that he stayed well hydrated. As a result, the team did NOT transport the patient, baby Robert, to the hospital as per protocol. Again, the established standard was to transport anyone and especially vulnerable populations (e.g. very young, elderly, homeless, etc.) to the emergency department, after being evaluated by the responding emergency medical technician, EMT or paramedics.

As a result of the bad weather, the crew had already worked a double shift. They had already made several thousand decisions before they arrived at baby Robert's house. The team was mentally and physically exhausted, to say the least.

Twelve hours later, the same paramedic crew was called back to the house for a "sick child." It was the same child, baby Robert. But this time, the child appeared clinically much sicker. The paramedic crew used the lights and siren of the ambulance to quickly transport the patient to the pediatric emergency department. The patient was pronounced dead several hours after arrival. It was determined that there was a delay in care.

The bottom line is that the providers were suffering from decision fatigue. They were mentally fatigued from all the decisions they had already contemplated. Meaning, they were not able to make optimal decisions, as a result, of all the previous decisions they had already established in the day.

Decision fatigue can occur in any industry and often increases with the height of the leadership position, or with the more people an individual is required to lead. Also, having direct involvement with these types of scenarios, regardless of the level of your position, may also increase the likelihood of decision fatigue. Can you think of examples when you suffered from decision fatigue?

Our brain is similar to a muscle. For instance, when we physically exercise our muscles, at some point, they become tired. And when your muscles become fatigued, they do not function as efficiently. A real-life example, would be marathon runners. Early in the race, their pace is strong, consistent, swift, naturally flowing, and effortless. We have all seen footage of marathon runners as the race progresses, the runner's stride is not optimal. It is inefficient, forceful, graceless, and requires a lot of energy unless you are a well-trained marathon runner, which 98% of the world is not. In short, the marathoner is fatigued and thus less efficient in his or her stride.

The brain functions the same way. Early in the day, your brain is refreshed and has plenty of energy and a great deal of thinking power. It can maximally process, synthesize enormous amounts of information and thus make reasonable and thoughtful decisions.

As the day progresses and as you make more decisions, your brain starts to tire. The brain experiences decision fatigue, which is the decline of your ability to make good decisions as you spend more time mulling over other decisions during the day. The more decisions you have to make, the sooner your brain becomes tired and thus functions less optimally.

In other words, the more daily decisions you need to make as the day goes on, the worse you become at weighing all the options and making educated choices.

There are a few famous people who live and act upon the concept of decision fatigue.

1. Former President Obama states, "You'll see I wear only gray or blue suits; I'm trying to pare down decisions. I don't want to make decisions about what I'm eating or wearing. Because I have too many other decisions to make…" Obama went on to explain, "the act of making a decision erodes your ability to make later decisions" **(Baer, 2014)**.
2. Mark Zuckerberg echoed that he has to serve a billion people and therefore does not want to waste energy on

minor decisions when there are larger impactful ones he needs to make. Mark wears the same grey t-shirt to trim down the number of smaller decisions that he has to make (Baer, 2015).

3. Steve Jobs wore the same blue jeans and black turtleneck every single day. He also wanted to limit the number of small decisions that he had to make.

In fact, an Israeli study looking at parole boards showed that convicts who appeared in front of the parole board earlier in the day were 65% more likely to be paroled compared to those who appeared later in the day and charged with similar crimes. The study re-enforced the importance and impact of decision fatigue.

Debra Cassens Weiss of the American Bar Association sums the study up well. The study found that board members were more likely to grant parole at the start of the day and after breaks for food. The problem, researchers said was, "choice overload." When faced with too many decisions, people are more likely to opt for the default choice. In these cases, the default was the "denial of parole." Meaning, when faced with too many decisions later in the day after already having made many decisions earlier in the day, the board did not have the energy to weigh all the options (Weiss, 2011).

There was another great study done at the University of Kent. The study had two groups. One group had to engage with a strenuous computer program for 90 minutes. The other group had to watch a neutral brain video for 90 minutes. Then both groups had to get on an exercise bike and pedal until they were fatigued enough to stop. Each group was allowed to choose its own resistance level.

One hundred percent of the time, the group who was not mentally drained (watched the neutral video) outperformed the mentally drained group. But what was more interesting is, each group chose the same resistance level for the bike ride. What that means is we are not very good at knowing when we are cognitively fatigued. Otherwise, the tired brain group would have chosen a more natural resistance (Baer, 2013).

Do you know when you are experiencing brain fatigue? Do you have strategies for preventing brain fatigue? And when brain fatigue occurs, what method(s) do you have in place to assist you during the period of fatigue?

One of the easiest and most common ways to assist with improving and staving off decision fatigue is to be sure that you are well-nourished. If your bloodstream sugar levels are low and thus your energy is low, then it is more likely that your brain level and energy levels will not be adequate, and you will, therefore, experience fatigue sooner.

In the next chapter, you will learn about a system that can be used, in order to, make it less likely that you will develop decision fatigue. It is mainly to be used when you are fatigued.

4

SPLIT-SECOND DECISIONS AND THE TLC FRAMEWORK

In March 2018, a flight attendant made a split-second decision, which ended up costing United Airlines an undisclosed amount of money in an out-of-court settlement and damaged their reputation. More importantly, a life, one family's ten-month-old puppy was lost due to the employee's decision. According to the breaking news from NPR, a flight attendant forced a woman who was traveling with her two young children and their family pet to stow her ten-month-old puppy, who was riding in a TSA-approved pet carrier, in the overhead bin because the carrier was slightly sticking out into the aisle.

During the three-plus hour flight, several passengers heard the dog barking, thus giving the flight attendant another chance to make a split-second decision, which could have had a positive outcome. She chose to keep the puppy locked away. Sadly, by the end, the carrier was deathly silent as the dog had suffocated in the tiny space. Imagine having to explain to your child that the noises heard throughout the flight were of your dog slowly dying by suffocation because you were forced to follow the rules of someone in authority. My question is this: What if the flight attendant had the proper training to make split-second decisions? Would there have been a positive outcome in this situation for the airlines, the family, the emotional well-being of the children and passengers present, and, most importantly, the puppy?

Application:

Teaching Good Leaders to Make Great Decisions

All decisions are not created equal. Some decisions are small, programmed, quick, routine, sudden, major, and minor, just to name a few. There are times that we have to make quick or spontaneous decisions. Then there are split-second decisions, too (to be discussed in great detail shortly). You have to be prepared for any type of decision, but especially split-second decisions.

It's not just the ER doctors and first responders who have to make life and death decisions (or merely critical decisions) on a daily, sometimes hourly basis. As suggested earlier, your business split-second decisions may not result in the death of a person. But they may result in the death of your company, the loss of contracts, employees, large amounts of money, time, and hiring of the wrong employees, just to name a few.

Consider the average CEO, vice president, manager, chief, etc. They are called upon to make split-second decisions regularly to put out fires with clients and staff, move the business forward, come from behind, and maintain positive relations. The point is we all make thousands of decisions each day, and thereby, we should know how important it is to understand, identify and eliminate the less important decisions to have a more productive and improved life.

Let's do the math for one year. If we make about 70 life-altering, life-impacting decisions every day, as I noted earlier, in 365 days, means we make 25,550 critical decisions annually. Of these decisions, 10,000 to 15,000 are split-second decisions. Split-second decisions are extremely high yield with maximum impact. Hence, if you want to epically and expeditiously improve your overall decision-making IQ, focus on optimizing your split-second decisions.

Training Your Mind For Split-Second Decisions

By maximally increasing your ability to make split-second decisions, you increase the ability to not only improve your life but improve the lives of those you lead, those who you interact with and your family's lives. We will be learning how to make split-second decisions and will include nuggets about decision-making overall.

In business and our personal lives, at times, we are asked to make decisions when there is not a perfect answer. Meaning, at times, there is not a right or wrong answer. Often you are merely choosing the "mostly right" decision. It is the decision that brings you closer to your next objective. Additionally, there may be times that you are called upon to make a decision from flawed or bad options, and you simply have to make the "most right" decision based on the information provided. But what is clear is that you have to make a decision. Not making a decision is a decision itself, which will be discussed in greater detail later.

You make many decisions all day. You make major and minor decisions. Minor decisions tend to require less thought; they tend to be routine and often do not have long term impact. Minor decisions may even seem important at the time but do not have much impact on the future. For instance, what color suit, which shoes, what time to schedule the weekly meeting, where the company retreat will be held, which office to give the new hire, where to go for lunch, where to shop, what dentist, where to get your executive MBA, what time to wake up on the weekends and the list goes on.

Whereas, major decisions often require longer thought, have long term impact, and there is usually a degree of difficulty in making the decision. For example, who and what talent to add to the team, who to promote, which measurable metrics for the organization to choose, resign from my stable job for a better long-term opportunity, spouse choice, where to buy a house, kids or no kids, if kids, where to send the kids to school and so on.

The minor and major decisions have a culminating impact over time. But the subcategory of significant decisions, split-second decisions, has the most immediate and significant impact in the short and long term. These decisions are where greatness is created. Or, if done poorly, lives are lost or destroyed; companies could be decimated. Knowing, understanding, and learning how to make split-second decisions will change your company's trajectory and your life beyond imagination.

Just as a side note, having interviewed many CEOs, chiefs of departments, and other executive-level people, what has become clear to me is that the leaders at the highest echelon tend to believe that they have a firm understanding and excellent split-second decision-making skills and they could be right. But great leaders always want to improve and grow their teams. Thus, they may not need additional leadership development, but their teams do.

Learning and studying to improve your split-second decision teaches good leaders to make great decisions. We only become better at what we repeatedly train and practice with high intention and focus.

Best-selling author and businessman Chet Holmes in his book, *The Ultimate Sales Machine*, shares a story about two woodcutters, "Woodcutter A cuts wood all day. Woodcutter B keeps stopping and sitting down. At the end of the day, woodcutter B has three times more wood than woodcutter A. Woodcutter A asks: 'How could this happen? You were resting all day!' Woodcutter B says: 'I wasn't resting. I was sharpening my saw,' Take time to sharpen your skills, your tools…"

The point is you must take time and train yourself and your teams on how to make split-second decisions. You have to keep your decision skills sharp. The sine qua non to improving your split-second decision ability is teaching and training. You have to teach what needs to be trained.

This is not about teaching you a complicated system that you will forget when you finish reading this book. It is about changing your life. The mission is to teach you a simple system that will grow you as a leader. It is about creating a thought process that will allow you to make momentous decisions for your organization. The goal is to keep it simple. As Albert Einstein said, "Everything should be as simple as possible, but not simpler." We want a digestible framework that we can regurgitate when needed. In fact, we want the split-second decision framework to become a natural part of your disciplined leadership thought process. It is about catapulting your company to new levels as a result of better split-second decisions. It is about improving your life and those you impact by improving your split-second decisions.

As an executive, often, our most significant concern, when we are not in the office, is what happens if something goes wrong. Knowing that your team has been trained to make split-second decisions will give you greater confidence in knowing that your team can handle the "stuff" that will go wrong.

To be sure that we are all on the same page, the working definition of split-second decisions that we will use moving forward are decisions that need to be made when there are time constraints, inadequate information, and significant or critical consequences as a result of the decisions.

The TLC Framework

To organize the split-second decision concept more succinctly, we will use the "TLC framework" for split-second decisions. No, the TLC does not stand for "tender, loving, care" in this book. It means Time, Lack of information, and Critical Consequences.

Split Second Decisions:

I) Time Constraint
II) Lack of Information
III) Critical Consequences

Again, the TLC framework means:

T - Time Contraints
L – Lack of Information
C – Critical Consequences

A decision that you simply feel rushed to make does not constitute a split-second decision. For instance, you may need to give the finance department your recommended budget for your department right away. But, in the end, the finance department is going to allocate money where needed. Meaning, your input is simply a helpful guide. This is not a split-second decision. Yes, you may feel pressure, but you are not making a split-second decision. There is not a time constraint, lack of information, or critical consequences. You are simply making decisions.

There is not one rule in life that captures all of everything. At best, we can plan for the Pareto Principle, which is the prediction that 80% of effects come from 20% of causes. Or a rule, a guideline, the outcome will not capture all the possible outcomes - only 80%. This means the TLC framework mostly captures 80% of split-second decisions. Yes, there are split-second decisions that will not fall under the TLC umbrella. You may or may not have all three components of split-second decisions, but critical consequences are a requirement. If you have all three components, you can be most likely assured that you are dealing with a split-second decision and need to be ready for action.

First Component: T, Time Constraint

Having spoken all over the world about split-second decisions, one common theme that people confuse is time. The feeling is that if you have a time constraint, are stressed or feel pressure, then you are making a split-second decision. Based on what we have learned thus far, a limited amount of time alone does not constitute a time split-second decision.

While the title is split-second decisions, the active variable is time. Many split-second decisions involve major time constraints that are longer than a few seconds. Therefore, the time constraint component sometimes has to be considered within *context*. So, if you usually have weeks to make a decision and you suddenly have to decide within hours, this could meet the requirement of the Time aspect of the TLC framework. There is a limited amount of time, just not seconds.

Time pressure is assumed whenever the time available for a task is shorter or perceived as being shorter than customarily required or reasonably expected. Meaning, there must be a lack of time and especially a sudden decrease in the amount of time that one would reasonably expect. While the unit of time will more often be in seconds, it could also be in minutes, hours, or even days. Another example, if you are suddenly told that you have to decide on the relative value unit that you will assign to projects in an attempt to decide which jobs will be eliminated, but you usually have weeks to have this number developed by close of business the next day, then this meets the definition of a time constraint as it relates to split-second decisions.

Additionally, when the unit of time is not in seconds, then there are those situations you may want to know the source of the time constraint in an attempt to assess if there is really a time constraint. How did the time constraint come about? Did you create it? Is it real?

Let's say that you are a parent with a critical meeting, and you are aiming to drop the kids off at school on time. As you are driving, Johnny, your eighth-grader, informs you that he's forgotten the permission slip for the annual eighth-grade graduation trip field trip and without it he won't be able to go. Now, while you no doubt find yourself in a bind, the decision you must make is not one that requires split-second thinking. Yes, if you return home for the permission slip, you will be late for the meeting you are hosting with top-level bosses. Yet there are more considerations to entertain, based on context, to guide our decision. Critically, you note, this is not a valid, time constraint because it is self-imposed. Johnny's school has, in the past, made allowances for similar rules. In this case, you know the teacher has set a deadline for the permission slips that were meant to give parents the same target. Therefore, you decide to bring Johnny to school without his permission slip and call the school before you arrive. Although, you may have needed to think quickly; it was not a split-second decision.

This is not a split-second decision. This is just a self-induced time constraint. Think about it. It is a senior trip that all eighth-graders go on. They know to count your child in the final numbers. The teacher or office has simply set a deadline for the expected time of the permission slips to be turned in.

Many rules are meant to provide guidance. They are mainly expected to give people the same target to meet. There are some rules intended for those who follow the rules. Are you a rule follower? Many of the greats are known for breaking the rules.

Again, time is a critical pillar in understanding split-second decisions. In many split-second decisions, you will be able to assess if the time constraint that has been placed on you is a true time constraint. Does the person or persons have the authority to place a time constraint on you or the situation?

For example, I had recently been appointed by the mayor of Washington, D.C., as the Medical Director and Assistant Chief for Fire and Emergency Medical Services for Washington, D.C., I was to report directly to the mayor. As an executive in the District of Columbia government, I was responsible for the acute management of all pre-hospital emergency medical care of everyone who needed care and transport in the District of Columbia. **Note:** Washington, D.C. swells to about 2 million people on weekdays and about 700,000 on nights and weekends.

My eighth day on the job and during a major snowstorm that stranded people at work, in vehicles and their homes, I received a call from a captain located at the central command requesting to "stop low acuity ambulance transports of citizens to hospitals until the environment is safer for the providers." This would put the decision of deciding who to transport and not transport in the wrong hands, and people could die. It was treacherous outside. The storm was so bad that it was named "Snowmageddon." Over 17 inches fell in less than 24 hours. I was on speakerphone and was informed that I needed to decide right then.

Admittedly, I had not been faced with such a situation in the past. So, I paused and said I would call them back in a few minutes. I sought advice from senior counsel within the department. As it turned out, he did not have the authority to make such a request of me. Furthermore, all he really wanted to know was if he should call in the second shift early. Had we stopped transporting low acuity patients, then there would be no need for him to call in the second shift early. The captain was under a time constraint, because he had only until a certain time to be able to call more staff in early. So in turn, he attempted to place a time constraint on me that he did not have the authority to do.

However, there were split-second decisions that needed to be made. I had to decide what to do about dwindling resources during the storm. I had not heard from my four captains who were on the streets, that would have been able to provide situation reports. And again, if we implemented the no transport of low acuity patients, there could be severe consequences for patients who we decided not to transport, that should have been transported.

Time constraints may not always be real and can be more than seconds, hours, or days. Context is everything.

Second Component: Lack of Information

The second pillar of split-second decisions is there not being enough information available for you to make an informed or optimal decision. Or maybe there is not enough specific information that you would generally have under normal conditions.

For example, in the emergency department during non-emergencies, before we give medications, we would generally have received a history of present illness, past medical history, review of systems, social history, surgical history, known drug allergies, vital signs, and physical exam. There are multiple people and many steps involved in acquiring the above standard information.

However, during what I would call a split-second decision moment or crisis, we may not have any of that crucial information, but yet still need to acutely give a patient medication. Let me share that I was the ER doctor working in the emergency department when the police arrived with the patient. The patient was a clean-cut, well dressed, and calm male who was presented in police custody. Let's name him Daniel. The police reported that "Daniel had been picked up in an area of the city that has a lot of drug traffic." The officer further stated, "Daniel was acting funny, not violent, but weird when we first engaged him. We decided to bring him to the emergency department for a psyche evaluation." The officers uncuffed Daniel so that we could take his vital signs and triage him. Daniel was cool and relaxed and gave his name and date of birth. Suddenly, Daniel stood up and said, "I am going to kill you" and lunged at the officers. A full fledge struggle ensued right in the ER. Daniel was unusually strong and violent - It took four people to restrain him.

I had to make a split-second decision to give Daniel medications without knowing his full history. I needed to inject him with 2 mg of Ativan, 5 mg of Haldol, and 50 mg of Diphenhydramine. The acute life-threatening concern was that I had no idea what he was allergic to. The wrong medication could cause him to have an acute drug reaction and perhaps experience anaphylactic shock and perhaps death.

Daniel was held down, and we injected him with the medications and strapped him to a stretcher. Fortunately, about a half-hour later, Daniel was calm and talking normally. He admitted to having had purchased PCP from a new distributor and thought that he had gotten a bad batch. Daniel did not develop any signs of allergic reactions or have any untoward reactions and was eventually discharged safely to his wife, who picked him up hours later. This is an example of not having the information you would like to have or are accustomed to having, while still needing to make a decision.

Let me assure you that not having enough information at times may make you feel powerless. As Sir Francis Bacon, an English philosopher, is credited for coining the concept, "information is power." In his own words, he writes, "Scientia potestas está" which translates to knowledge is power. Now, do not read too deeply into it. Simply put, information is power. But a lack of it does not make you powerless. You still have to perform and make decisions. In other words, you have to use what you have, to get things done.

As we all know, information is power. But a lack of information does not make you powerless. It also does not absolve you of the responsibility of making a decision. You still have to perform. You still must make decisions. You must use what is available to you at that time and decide.

And at times, your decision is going to be wrong. For instance, in the case above with Daniel, what if I have given medicine that caused an allergic reaction? I needed to be prepared to make the next decision. What is my point? Regardless of the outcome of your first decision, you must be prepared to make your next decision. We will discuss this later.

Third Component: Critical Consequences

The severity of any consequence is both relative and proportional to the impact of a decision. What is severe often depends on context: to what extent can we or others be harmed by our split-second decision?

Say a mother is being asked on the spot if her sixteen-year-old daughter can drive back home with her best friend, who only recently received her driver's license. There are many factors to consider and as many potential consequences. The mother doesn't know if the best friend has been in any accidents, or even if she is a good driver. She doesn't know whose car it is or whether the car has recently been serviced. The mother, on the other hand, is familiar with teenage driving statistics:

- Drivers ages fifteen to twenty years old make up 6.7% of the total driving population, but are involved in 35% of all crashes and accidents.
- An average of nine teens are killed in car accidents every day.
- The risk of an accident increases drastically by having another teen in the car while a teen is driving (many states do not allow new drivers to have other teens in the car).

• The likelihood of sudden death goes up as much as 50% once a teen gets their license.

What does a mother do in this situation? Worst case scenario, the mother's daughter stands the chance of dying in an accident. Or she could also suffer a severe injury or any number of other misfortunes. And at best, the daughter could make it home alive.

All split-second decisions are not equal. Even in the earlier example with Daniel, the consequences of giving him the wrong medications could have been the most severe of all, death. A significant or severe consequence, in the context of split-second decisions, is one that would lead to irrevocable harm, damage, change or significant loss. The wrong decisions you make in a split-second could impact your career, devastate your finances, cost your company to lose millions or harm your family and/or business or even cause the harm or death of others.

The definition of severe consequences is enough, but it is not exhaustive. There is a great deal of context and circumstances surrounding critical consequences. What may be severe in one company may not be considered severe in another company. This is true individually too. What may be severe to you may not be severe to someone else.

A good example would be two deaths, I experienced while working in the ER. In both cases, the patients were elderly; one patient was 99 years old, and the other was 102 years old.

The 102-year-old patient presented to the ER in the ambulance with the report that the patient had stopped responding and had a very slow heart rate. The family was present and shared, "We have known for a while that this day was coming and are prepared for whatever happens but want you to do everything possible." The ER team and I did everything possible, yet the patient died 30 minutes after arrival. I pronounced her dead at 10:13 a.m. and had a family meeting from 10:15 a.m. – 10:25 a.m.

At the end of the meeting, the family shared with me that they were "going to go back to work and that the funeral would be within five days." I was surprised that they were going back to their respective jobs, and I guess that my expression showed it. The son of the deceased lady then said, "My mother prepared us when she first got sick. And she said, 'The consequence of living is always death. So, please be happy that I had a good life and have moved on'." Admittedly, the son had a certain calm and confidence.

In the case of the 99-year-old, she came in by ambulance as well. She had stopped eating days before arrival and reportedly had several low blood pressure readings the days leading up to transport. This patient also had several family members. During her ER stay, the patient's pulse started to drop, and her blood pressure lowered as well. We had to move her to the resuscitation room.

The family started to scream and say, "Please do not let her die." Unfortunately, after heroic efforts, I pronounced the patient dead at 4:12 p.m. I met with the family at 4:15 p.m., and the meeting did not end until 5:02 p.m. (of course, I had to leave the room several times to tend to other patients). But the one family leader said, "…What are we going to do? She is dead. What are we to do?" The entire family was distraught and did not leave the ER until after 9:30 p.m.

What is the point of telling these two stories? At times, consequences and the interpretation of consequences are relative and may even require a context. In both of these cases, the result was death, but it appeared to be more severe to the less prepared family. In short, consequences are often viewed through the lens of persons or companies that have to interpret or experience the severity of the consequences.

Also, consequences should be considered in terms of the individual organization or person. For example, I was at my daughter's softball game and talked with her coach. The upcoming Rock and Roll Marathon came up; it was a week away. I had a few friends who were training for it. I shared, "Too bad the marathon registration was closed; otherwise, I would consider running it even at this late date." Although my regular running regimen consisted of eight to ten mile runs five times a week, I was in no way prepared to run a marathon. I was only joking.

Do you know, the coach said, "I am in charge of the marathon, and I can get you in... do you want to do the half or the full marathon?" A half marathon is 13.1 miles, and a full marathon is 26.2.

A week later, I was running the Rock and Roll Marathon and was at the 13.0-mile mark, and physically I was feeling good. I had to make the split-second decision to turn left and complete the half marathon in the next two hundred yards. Or I could continue straight and attempt to complete the entire marathon while simultaneously complaining the next two hours while running about why I decided to do the whole race.

I chose to complete the entire marathon. It was a split-second decision for me, mainly because of the severe long-term consequences. Had I not done the entire race, I would have spent the next year asking myself, daydreaming, and wondering why I did not do the entire race. At some point, I would have decided to do the next race and appropriately trained. Adequately training for a marathon requires an enormous amount of time. It would take a great deal of time away from my business and family, and from my perspective, those were severe consequences.

The point is there are "critical consequences" that we understand that do not need a context, (i.e., loss of jobs, multimillion-dollar contracts, life, money, etc.) to understand or feel the immediate impact. But then there are those "critical consequences" which are relative, but very real to the individual or to a specific company.

Putting It All Together

Story:

We were sitting in the break room of the emergency department and happened to see on the local news that there was a house fire, and there appeared to be many victims. We had not received a call from the emergency medical dispatch services, so we were not too concerned. As we sat there and finished our lunch, the nurse came to tell me that the radio ambulance dispatch was on the phone.

"This is paramedic Smith Engine 109. We will be there in approximately five minutes, and onboard we have a young male critically injured from a house fire, which we had to intubate. We are bringing four additional patients, also. I am requesting more pain medication." You could hear the urgency and stress in the ambulance provider's voice. Before I could give orders for additional sedation medicine, we lost reception.

We all got up to prepare the resuscitation equipment needed for burn patients. While preparing before the ambulances had arrived with the burn patients, the nurse came and said, "Doctor, there is a patient in triage who walked in from the fire. He appears to be high off something." I asked the nurse to put the patient in a room, and I would run and see him before the critical patients arrived.

The patient was a short-medium build male with a mustache who appeared unkempt and possibly homeless. Let's call him Peter. He smelled like smoke. Peter informed us that he had been in a fire, but came to be checked out. Peter was slow to respond. His pupils were slightly constricted, and he was showing signs of what experienced medical providers would call the "heroin nod." A heroin nod patient is intoxicated from heroin and often nods off while answering questions. I was finally able to gather that Peter had been in a house fire and was stuck in the house until the fire department arrived. He said, "There was smoke everywhere when they got me out." Peter said they took him to the ambulance, but then he saw his brother and decided to just have his brother drive him to the hospital.

As I was obtaining a brief history, the nurse interrupted to say that the first burn victim was there, and I really needed to come to the trauma bay. I quickly asked a few more poignant questions (I did not acquire and adequate history or do a physical exam - lack of information). During the history, Peter said, "I feel fine, but I am coughing more now than I did before the fire." I did not notice if Peter had soot, a black powdery substance, in his mouth and nasal airway. Soot is made up of incomplete burned particles. Soot in a patient's mouth is a sign of significant smoke exposure in the mouth and throat, often causing irritation. Irritation leads to swelling in the mouth, which leads to airway compromise. Complete airway compromise leads to death.

In between more severe patients, I went back to quickly talk to Peter. I noticed that he was coughing more but was not in distress. In a split-second, I made the decision not to secure Peter's airway and go and tend to the incoming patients.

While tending to the patients who the ambulance and firefighters brought in, the nurse came and said, "You need to see patient Peter right now."

When I walked in, Peter was blue. His oxygen level had dropped to 74% (It was and should be 100%). Peter was dying. We called for additional help. I looked in Peter's mouth; his airway was almost completely closed from the irritation of the soot. I gave Peter a sedative so that I could place a breathing tube down his mouth so I could secure his airway and allow him to breathe. I failed on the first attempt. I was not able to see anything because of the swelling. Peter's oxygen level had reached deficient levels that would not sustain his life if I could not get the tube down his mouth and into his trachea. The nurse bought the intubation blade that had a video camera attached. Now, I could see his airway with the camera and was successfully able to place the endotracheal tube that allowed Peter to breathe.

Peter was admitted to the ICU. He did well and was discharged home in normal condition.

1. **Time** – There was not enough time to gather enough information at the beginning. There were time constraints as it related to placing the tube.
2. **Lack of Information** – I did not know if soot was in Peter's mouth. Had I known that soot was present, I would have chosen a different course of action. Additionally, I did know that it was a drug-infested house where the fire had taken place, and Peter had just used heroin before the fire.
3. **Consequences, Severe** – The entire ordeal could have led to the loss of human life.

I made the wrong split-second decisions. When I heard Peter coughing, I should have made a different decision that would not have led to a life-threatening situation. Had I applied the split-second decision framework while providing for Peter, I would not have found myself in the acute life-threatening situation.

Practical Use:

Rarely do we consciously expect to make split-second decisions. And yet we know that they come several times a day and at any time. Simply recognizing and understanding the framework of split-second decisions improves your ability to make them. You must train yourself to be prepared to make many of the most important decisions of your day. Directly stated, if you improve your split-second-decision-making ability, then you improve your entire life, which includes your business life too.

There is a poem by an unknown author that says, "Life isn't measured by the number of breaths you take, but by the number of moments that take your breath away." Understanding that split-second decisions are your most important decisions, I created a poem for you: life is not measured by the number of decisions you make; it is measured by the number of split-second decisions you get right.

5

MINDSET NEEDED FOR SPLIT-SECOND DECISIONS

We all hear about mindset. I asked several people what mindset meant. I received different answers from each one. Many were deep and complicated. For example, is a person's mindset fixed or can it be changed? Or is our mindset always evolving? Again, in the true spirit of Albert Einstein, "Everything should be made as simple as possible, but not simpler." The easy and functional definition of the mindset that we will use moving forward is a set of beliefs or attitudes you hold about your company and yourself and you and your company's abilities. And a company and person can change their mindset.

As it relates to split-second decisions, one component of the overall mindset that must be present is what we will refer to as the "whatever it takes" or WIT motto . The intention and focus are on completing, accomplishing, or succeeding at whatever goal you have set no matter what. Yes, that is probably too intense for a few. But take a deep breath. The relief is YOU control your mindset, and YOU define success.

Nugget - There are a few truths we must accept:

1. The road to success is NEVER straight with no pivots.
2. The journey to accomplishment is not the same for everyone.
3. There will be, at a minimum, emotional pain, if not physical pain as well.

Success is a set of goals that, at times, are pliable and yielding. They bend and stretch as circumstances dictate. Once you achieve your initial measure level of success, there is always something in the distance that will reveal itself to you that you will then want. And that gives birth to another goal or pathway needed to be created.

Additionally, success must be considered within context. The environment, circumstances, life events, and what is going on around you must all be appropriately weighted. For example, if you wear a suit to work every day, that is fine. However, if you change environments and it is a hot summer Saturday afternoon at the park, you may appear strange or out of place with a suit on. Hence, context plays an important role.

In reality, our success is most often temporary. For instance, if you are an undergraduate first year student, success may be completing your first year with a 3.9 GPA. As you matriculate and start to move towards graduation, success may be to be hired by a Fortune 500 corporation, or perhaps your goal is to be accepted into medical school or even a jet engineer.

Once hired by a large corporation, your next measure of success will likely be to become a supervisor, then a manager, and then a director. As your successes grow, you will likely raise or change your definition of success. You may later define success as being appointed vice-president, senior vice-president, and subsequently CEO or President of a company. Your definition of success will change again. Most importantly, success is not a singular event. It is a series of events, actions, and measurable outcomes that grow you and change how you define success. Success becomes temporary, based on events and context.

You have to do what is referred to as "fail your way to success."

Success is never a straight line upward. There will always be setbacks or what some call failures. Or will there be failures? In the "whatever it takes" space, there is no such thing as failure. Why? Because "whatever it takes," (i.e. WIT) is inclusive of failure. Failure is a requirement for success. If failure is a pre-requisite for success, then is it a failure? No, it is not. It is a crucial component of achievement. It is a matter of perspective. In the WIT world, there are no failures or losses. There are only lessons. I'll say it again, if failure is required for success, and there are no failures or losses in the WIT world, then there are only lessons, and thus you never fail.

Let's be clear. This is not a play on words. This is a mindset requirement of WIT. We do not experience losses in WIT, we experience lessons. We only grow and learn. We take our lessons learned from the experiences of what others call failures and losses and use them as our repertoire of knowledge to draw from to move us towards epic success.

Another vital component of epic success is emotional pain. Yes, there will be pain. To keep it simple, pain is the "stuff" that hurts on the inside. No band-aid or pill can fix it. "Stuff" is a requirement of success too. There is not one successful person who did not have to endure pain. You know there is pain coming, so you will not be paralyzed by it when it comes. You will be better positioned to move forward. The faster you can learn the lessons that pain has taught you, the sooner you can move forward to massive achievement.

Ask yourself, "What is my mindset, and what do I need to do to improve it?"

My Story

Are you born great, or does life make you great? The school bell rang, and it was time to take inventory of my courage. However, there was not much to inventory; either I had to fight or get beat up.

I grew up stuttering since birth. It was not until my thirties that I could speak well enough that those around me did not know I had a speech impediment. As a result of the stuttering at school, and in any new environment, I drew the attention of the bully. At that stage of my life, it was unwanted attention. It came with teasing, malicious comments and looks of unwanted sympathy. It also came with a lot of fighting. Back in those days, it was the typical fist fights and wrestling. No one really tried to hurt anyone. I lost some and won some, but these life events truly created the spirit of the fight in me.

As a result of the class being small and intimate, when I stuttered, things seemed worse than having to get beat up. Many times, when I was called to answer a question in class, I would stutter my way through the answer. Students would often laugh and interrupt me as I stuttered – especially the long stutters and explain why they thought that my answer was wrong. Yes, I had done my homework. But the long pauses during my stutters created a space that people felt compelled to fill with their voice.

Interestingly, no matter what, in each class, when I was right or even close to the right answer, the teacher(s) would often explain why I was right. He/She would sometimes interrupt the student that had interrupted me. It happened so often that I came to expect my answer to be right. What the other students and I did not know was that this was a subtle way the teachers showed support to me.

Nevertheless, I came to expect to be right. It became part of my framework. And I was right so often that it indirectly encouraged me to speak up more and answer more questions. Why? I had no fear of being wrong. And if I was wrong. No big deal.

Remarkably, the stuttering allowed me to hide in plain sight. As a result of the stutter, many who did not know me protected and encouraged me. A lot of teasing took place before and after school on the playground. Yet, I really loved playing on the playground, especially in the morning.

While in elementary school, I remember that it was time to apply for the job of doing morning and after school announcements over the loudspeaker. There were three positions available. This entire experience changed me. I told my mother and father, who both practiced with me a great deal at home. We discussed what our family celebration would be, once I earned the speaking position.

And then, when I went to school, the principal called all the applicants to the office for auditions. Many of the students were laughing at me for even applying for the position. While waiting, the principal came out boldly and said, "Geoff, I saw you run that touchdown on the playground this morning. You are different. It looks like you have a really good chance of getting one of the speaker positions., but you know that you will have to give up your morning playground time."

In the end, I was not chosen for any of the speaking positions. But the principal anointing me as worthy changed my standing amongst the other students. In fact, that same week, it was announced over the loudspeaker that I had been given the biggest position that everyone wanted in the Thanksgiving school play. I got to be the shark. It was a non-talking position that EVERYONE wanted because of the costume. The principal and teacher had chosen me.

Next, I was inexplicably chosen to be a school patrol. You know the ones who got to wear the red or yellow crossing guard belt and were allowed to leave class early to help with dismissal. I was also chosen to be the captain of the crossing guards. I got to wear a captain's badge.

What is the point? At a very young age, I was anointed with a mindset that greatness is me, not fear of failure, and I had an expectation to be right.

Greatness and leadership go hand in hand. What experiences have you had that have shaped the expectation of your future? Write down the top three experiences that have shaped your leadership trajectory. Then write down the experiences that you need to take you to the next level.

Finally, tell yourself the mindset needed for your next leadership position.

What is *mindset*? Mindset is a collection of conscious and unconscious beliefs that you have about yourself based on your past failures and successes. There is great debate around if your beliefs are permanent or can be changed. A full discussion surrounding this subject is outside the scope of this book. But this chapter is written

Training Your Mind For Split-Second Decisions

from the vantage point that mindsets can be changed to meet the needs of the individual.

Good news. Simply, based on the fact that you have chosen to read this book suggests that if you do not already possess the following three required mindset criteria, then you will be able to develop them rapidly.

1. **You must expect to be right.**

No matter what has happened to you in your life, you are in your position for a reason. At this time, at this moment, on this day, in this year, you have been placed to make split-second decisions and/or make multiple decisions. Decide with the intention and expectation of being right.

Often when we are deciding, there is not a perfect decision. But from the onset, you should expect to be as right as possible. If you enter the decision thinking you are going to be wrong, then you will likely be wrong. Confucius once said, "The man or woman who thinks they can and the man or the woman who think they can't are probably both right." You are most likely correct.

1. **You must not have fear of being wrong.**

The most common reason why people fail to make decisions, and thus split-second decisions, is due to their fear of being wrong. Often this fear is rooted in concern of what other people are going to think of you if you are wrong or the possible consequences. The consequences will be the consequences, no matter what. The fear that you impose simply delays or distracts you from your decision.

Back to what others think. If you make the wrong decision, you feel that they are judging you based on what they think they know about you. The truth is all they may know is that the decision you made did not have the desired outcome. Matter-of-factly, you do not know about their bad decisions. And everybody has made several. You just do not know about how they were wrong in their decisions.

Nugget: What other people think about you is none of your business. Why? You can't control what someone else thinks. They view the world through their own lens.

Additionally, when you are fearful about your decisions, you often preemptively strategize excuses for your wrong decisions. What do I mean? Instead of giving something your best, you may only give it 80%, and then if it does not work out, you can fall back on, "I did not give it my best."

Let's look at it differently. You make a decision, and it was "wrong." Then your decision puts you in the category of the greats:

- Walt Disney made hundreds of bad decisions that caused him to go bankrupt multiple times.
- Oprah Winfrey is famous for saying, "I have made the greatest number of wrong decisions."
- Stephen King decided what went into his first several hundred book proposals, which were all rejected.
- Stephen Jobs was fired from Apple for countless wrong split-second decisions.
- Martin Luther King had a March on Albany, New York that failed miserably before there was the famous March on Washington in 1963.

What is my point? Making the wrong decisions is a requirement for success. Anyone who all their decisions are correct, is not making enough decisions.

1. **Greatness is in you.**

As the motivational speaker Les Brown has stated, "You do not have to be great to start, but you have to start to be great."

You must believe greatness is in you. If you believe that you are great, you are less fearful about life as a whole.

If for some reason you find yourself falling short in your feeling of greatness, do what we all do at various times, develop an alter ego. For example, think about that quiet and mild mannered mid-level manager who keeps to himself, but when leadership makes an unreasonable demand of his subordinates, he musters the courage to speak up like a lion in their best interest. Or what about that quiet, insecure, and scared parent who cowards to most people, but yet will roar or fight like a bear when it comes to protecting their children. My point is, we all have an alter ego that we just have to know how and when to bring out.

I am going to give you an alter ego to use when necessary. Your alter ego is Gabrielle. You are strong and fearless. You do not mind being wrong, and failure is not an option. Hence, every time you are wrong or perhaps failed, you recognize that the resultant lessons and insights learned bring you closer to greater success. If you are not failing at anything or you are always right, it means you are not trying hard enough, or you are making meaningless decisions.

Gabrielle also accepts that it is what it is. Based on the information available to you at that moment, you decided and did what you thought was appropriate. Nobody is perfect, so do not put the burden of perfection on yourself.

Another way of saying this is: Accept that you are not God. You will be wrong. The following four situations are very likely:

1. You were given the necessary information but made a wrong decision.
2. You did not have all the information and made the wrong decision.
3. You had the wrong information and made the wrong choice.
4. You had all the information needed and made the right decision, but it did not give the expected results.

What is the point? No matter how experienced, informed, aware, studied, talented of a leader that you are, you will be wrong at times.

But this is where greatness is improved and/or made. Do not fear being wrong. It is necessary for greatness.

There is not a set number of wrong decisions that you have to make on the road to greatness. There is not even a rule about the number of consecutive times that you will be wrong. But as long as you have your mindset on greatness and do not quit, your path will be fulfilling and rich. You will be an asset to your organization or perhaps your next organization. But again, no matter what, do not quit.

Poet John Greenleaf Whittier sums up the reasons not to quit very well in his poem, "Don't Quit."

> When things go wrong as they sometimes will,
> When the road you are trudging seems all uphill,
> When the funds are low and the debts are high,
> And you want to smile, but you have to sigh,
> When care is pressing you down a bit,
> Rest if you must but don't you quit.
> Life is strange with its twists and turns
> As every one of us sometimes learns
> And many a failure turn about
> When he might have won had he stuck it out;
> Don't give up though the pace seems slow—
> You may succeed with another blow.
> Success is failure turned inside out—
> The silver tint of the clouds of doubt,
> And you never can tell just how close you are,
> It may be near when it seems so far.
> So, stick to the fight when you're hardest hit—
> It's when things seem worst that you must not quit.

PRACTICAL APPLICATION:

You never lose. You may not win, but you never "lose." You learn lessons. If "failure" or "losses" are requirements for success, then you never lose or fail. You have already learned that people must "fail or lose" their way to greatness.

As a side note, in no way am I saying that you ever enter into a decision or situation expecting to be wrong or to fail. Hence, that would go against the laws of nature that we have discussed in this book.

6
PREPARING FOR SPLIT-SECOND DECISIONS

Story

It was early spring, but still cold and rainy. I was working the early shift. The rain had caused a lot of motor vehicle accidents. The ER had received several patients who were involved in MVCs. A few presented as trauma patients and had to be either admitted to the intensive care unit or taken to the operating room for an emergency procedure.

I was asked to evaluate a priority four patient, meaning a low acuity patient. This was someone who was not going to require a lot of ER resources and would very likely be discharged.

The triage note stated that the patient was a 44-year-old male who had been involved in a low-speed MVC a few days ago and presented with back pain. The patient had been seen at an outside ER and had been given pain medicine with no improvement.

I walked into the room and introduced myself as the ER doctor who would be taking care of him. Let's name the patient Joel. Joel was a healthy looking 44-year-old male, laying on the stretcher with a young woman rubbing his head. Joel was in no acute distress.

Both Joel and his lady friend identified themselves as being in the health care field. They both began to speak and shared that Joel had been in a low-speed MVC five days ago, and there was minimal damage to the car with no airbag deployment. The lady had been in the car but did not have any pain.

Joel confided that he had been seen at an outside urgent care facility who had told him that he had whiplash. They prescribed an anti-inflammatory, a muscle relaxant, and a narcotic. Joel thought that he needed more pain management and a few more days off from work before he could return.

I assessed that this was just another wimpy male who had been involved in a fender bender and could not handle pain, especially with his lady friend hovering over him as if he were seriously injured.

In my 20 years of practicing medicine, I have come to understand that overall, men do not deal with minor pain well. And if there is a significant other, they manage to overstate the pain.

I took a history and did a physical exam. As expected, Joel had some slight lower back muscle spasms but no bony tenderness. Clinically, Joel did not appear to be in much pain.

After my exam, I discussed the case with Joel. I said that it appeared that he had a muscle spasm with whiplash. I let him know that I was going to give him a work excuse for three more days and give him a script for Percocet and more muscle relaxants. I told him I thought he just needed more time to heal. Joel agreed, and I started to leave the room to prepare his discharge papers.

Just as I was leaving, I heard Joel say to his friend, "Looks like I won't be able to run again tomorrow". Me being an avid runner, I turned around and asked how far he ran each day. He said about seven miles. "How long have you been running?" Joel said, "About 20 years." Then Joel mentioned all the marathons and 10k's that he had participated in. I asked him when was the last time he had gone for a run. Joel said, "Five days ago, the day before the accident. I have not gone more than two days without running in years."

Now, I became slightly more concerned because being a long-distance runner of over 20 years, I know that when it comes to a dedicated runner, they never miss too many days. Personally, I know people who were late for their own wedding because they had to run.

So, for a staunch runner to not run for several days was extremely abnormal. I said to them, "I am sure that it is nothing, but since you are here, why don't we get an x-ray of your back." The x-ray was abnormal, so the radiologist recommended a CT scan, which is a better test. The CT came back completely abnormal, and the radiologist called and recommended a stat MRI.

As it turns out, Joel had a "pathologic fracture" of his thoracic area. He had an advanced form of cancer. The car accident may have saved Joel's life. We did more tests; I called the oncologist, and the patient was admitted and had started chemotherapy before I left the hospital.

Joel and his lady friend were distraught. They did not understand how the urgent care had missed his fracture. I explained that Joel had a classic presentation of whiplash secondary to a low-speed MVC. The urgent care physician's treatment and discharge medicine were reasonable.

I then reminded them that I was about to discharge them too. The only thing that had prevented that was the fact that I was a runner. I had also read an article about a guy who came to the ER for a horrible leg fracture simply from walking down steps. And as it turned out, he had bone cancer, which made his leg weak. Without the leg fracture, the gentleman would have never come to the ER.

I also shared with them that I had a great meditation session that morning, which made me unusually more patient and calmer. It was that patience that made me ask about the running.

I further admitted to the patient and female friend that me getting the right diagnosis had nothing to do with my clinical skills or my depth of medical knowledge. We were both fortunate that I was a runner who had a great deal of patience that day who had read an article in a non-science magazine about someone being saved as a result of a fortunate pathologic fracture.

Application:

Preparing for Your Split-Second Decisions

Many of your split-second decisions have already been decided well in advance. Meaning, when we are placed in a time-pressured and stressful situation, we tend to thin slice. We use little information to make big assumptions and conclusions. We make judgments, decisions, and split-second decisions about particular circumstances, matters, or persons based on whatever details are in front of us at that current time. But what is the basis for our findings?

It is time for a quick discussion on conscious, subconscious, and unconscious. The vast majority of work discussed and written about conscious, sub-conscious, and unconscious stems from Sigmund Freud's psychoanalytic theory of personality. In short, the conscious mind includes everything that is in our awareness. It includes what we see, hear, touch, smell, and think. For example, it is your conscious mind that is reading this book.

Our subconscious is that part of our mind that operates without our direct awareness, and we have very little active control. It is often influenced by our experiences. While the subconscious mind is resistant to change, it is malleable. Examples of your subconscious mind would be memories, beliefs, painful experiences, and many other subjective interpretations of your experiences. Consider the subconscious mind as the storage center for all of our past experiences and memories that we do not have conscious direct easy access to. An example of the subconscious:

You lose your keys, and you are looking for them all over the house. But you can't find them. So, you are getting frustrated and upset. You try hard to think, but you just can't recall where they are. Then you sit down, and something distracts you. Then, at that moment, you remember, "The keys are right on the desk to the left of the TV!"

What happened there? You were consciously trying to remember where your keys were and couldn't, but then your mind focused on something else, while your subconscious mind kept working on looking for your keys. Get it? This actually happens all the time and to every one of us daily (Daniels, 2015).

Your unconscious mind is that part of our brain that is not known to our conscious mind. It is that part of our mind that is automatic. We do not think about it. It includes past traumatic events, socially unacceptable thoughts, and behaviors. Most of what is in our unconscious mind is socially unacceptable, undesirable and unpleasant. For a good example of unconscious bias, we can just look at a resume for example:

"This candidate sounds excellent!" Resumes are a consistent source of unconscious bias. One particular study gave a group of managers a set of resumes. Some of them were exact duplicates where only the names had been changed. Resumes with the Anglo sounding names received substantially more callbacks than those with diverse names of other origins. Clearly, it was the names and their associated biases that impacted the decisions instead of the qualifications and value they could bring to the company.

Activities were another source of assumptions. Those that sounded more prestigious, like polo or horseback riding vs. basketball or softball, skewed the perception of the candidates. Those engaged in more prestigious sounding activities were considered more refined and successful than their counterparts simply because of their perceived financial status. These conclusions may have very well been valid, but they could have just as easily been untrue. An interviewer's bias makes a substantial difference in the selection arena. Very talented applicants would have been turned away for unfounded reasons (Eli Inc., 2016).

In sum, we are products of your past experiences. This includes the good, the bad, and the ugly and past experiences that impact our split-second decisions. What we will learn in this book will allow us to utilize our conscious, subconscious, and subconscious pre-dispositions to optimize and improve our split-second decisions.

The people we choose to associate with, what we read, our "blind spots", our ability to meditate, and our fitness regimens all have unique roles in our split-second decisions. Let's start with "blind spots" or what many would call our inherent biases.

Blind Spots

Blind spots are attitudes or leanings that unconsciously affect our decisions and actions. Yes, we have all heard about implicit bias as it refers to race. But the fact is we all, including objective professionals, (i.e., judges, doctors, law enforcement, lawyers, etc.) have "blind spots" or biases about almost everything.

A good example comes from the medical world and women with heart disease. The literature is unequivocal that women who present with similar signs and symptoms as men as it relates to an acute coronary event, also known as heart attacks, are overwhelmingly treated less aggressively. Unless you think that physicians across the nation have conspired to purposely agree to treat women who present with similar heart attack symptoms less aggressively, then this is a clear example of a "blind spot" or implicit bias. Most biases are unconscious and the perpetrator is not aware. And those biases impact our decisions and our split-second decisions.

Furthermore, your bias is amplified when you are stressed, have less time, or when you are distracted. Hence, your blind spots are in full effect while making split-second decisions. Not having any biases is virtually impossible. In fact, I would be very wary of people and especially leaders who state that they do not have biases. If you have not identified your biases, you can take the Harvard implicit bias test, https://implicit.harvard.edu/implicit/.

An excerpt from the NPR podcast entitled, "How The Concept of Implicit Bias Came Into Being" radio guest, Yale and Harvard professor and psychologist, Dr. Mahzarin Banaji, sums bias up this way:

"To just think about where implicit bias comes from, it's a good idea to think about it as a combination of two things. First, our brains - human brains have a certain way in which we go about picking up information, learning it. If I repeatedly see that doctors are male and nurses are female, I'm going to learn that. But the second part to implicit

bias is the culture in which we live. There is a culture that, for whatever reasons, has led to men being surgeons and women being nurses. If I lived in a culture where the opposite happened, I would have the opposite bias. When we discover things about ourselves or the world, that's new, we have to expect the kind of reaction that we're getting. But the mark of an evolved society is how quickly do we come to terms with it?

How quickly do we realize that finding out that we're biased need not mean that we have to remain biased? So, I have great hope just because I look at the history of this country, where we used to be and where we are today, and I see nothing but a path that is on the way towards doing better" (Montagne, 2016).

Let's be clear. There is no way to completely rid yourself of all your "blind spots", but you can either own your biases or not let them own you. Being able to identify your own and becoming self-aware of your "blind spots" allows you a more deliberate role in the impact of the bias. Also, being able to identify and adjust your thinking as a result of the bias is taking complete ownership, but for the sake of this book, the best quick way to minimize the impact "blind spots" has on your decision-making is to recognize that you have them.

There is another term that we must be familiar with, neuroplasticity. It is the physiologic, histologic, and gross changes that occur to your brain as a result of interacting with the environment. More clearly, your brain can physically change as a result of your experiences. The brain is made up of trillions of neurons and connections. Let's look at these neuronal connections as railroad tracks. One decision is linked to thousands of tracks. For example, if you want a drink of water, there are several neuronal pathways in your brain that tells you how to get a drink of water. If you want to get up every morning at 4:00 a.m., there is a pathway linked to getting up early.

You can change those tracks. It is the essence of neuroplasticity. Your brain can form new pathways as a result of interactions with the environment. More excitingly, science has learned that we can purposely create tracks. We can create tracks that help with our split-second decisions.

A good example of this would be a new snowfall and driving. Have you ever been the first to drive on the road after a heavy snowfall? The first car, for safety reasons, has to go slow. It is creating a track. The next car has to go slow as well because that car is creating a track too. But as each subsequent car travels that same road, each car can begin to go faster because there are tracks or pathways to follow. But the exciting part is we can choose the paths we want and lay down new tracks. Hence, you can lay the pathway that you will need for your split-second decisions. Thus, you will have a quicker response to your split-second decision.

I am not suggesting that we know all of the split-second decisions that are coming our way. What I am saying is that it is essential to have tracks laid as a framework, as a part of the process, for making good split-second decisions. A good example of laying focused tracks for a scenario that you do not know the specifics for would be the military. For example, all branches of the military train for war. All branches train on basic and specific skills: military discipline, physical fitness, first aid, and a host of other skills. They are creating tracks. However, even in doing so the armed services, the majority of the time, still does not know the specifics of the 5 W's; when, where, why, who, and what in regards to the war. However, service members are better prepared because they have laid the groundwork for tracks. Imagine sending our armed forces to war with no tracks. As part of our leadership obligation to our organizations, families, and selves, we must have firmly laid tracks for making split-second decisions. The TLC framework provides an important and necessary foundation.

Yes, without any type of surgery, we are going to change our brains. We are going to lay down new neuronal tracks and literally change the histological structure of our brain.

Principle:

There are five extremely high yield areas that, with great focus and intentionality, you can impact over time that will allow you to lay new pathways and thus dramatically not only improve our split-second decisions but to optimize them as well.

1. Reading, focused
2. People
3. Blind Spots or Experiences
4. Meditation
5. Fitness

"Show me their reading list and you will reveal the person and their success or the lack thereof..."
- Anonymous

PREPARING FOR SPLIT-SECOND DECISIONS

1. READING

What you read and the people you associate yourself with for years, months, weeks, days, or even hours leading up to your split-second decision, will have a profound impact on how those decisions play out. Developing a daily reading routine puts you in a better position to make the best decision at that moment.

Deliberate and focused reading gives your conscious and subconscious a significantly larger pool of knowledge from which to draw. Reading increases the swiftness and dexterity of your brain. It allows you to marry the contents of the book with your interpretation of what's written, then be steeped in your pool of experiences. All of a sudden, you have three times as much information to make a withdrawal from your fund of information for your split-second decisions.

Eighty-eight percent of the most accomplished and financially successful people read about 30 minutes a day. Let there be no doubt that there is a direct correlation between reading, decision-making, and success. The greater number of big decisions that you get right, the more successful you are. And now we have learned that it is specifically the greater number of split-second decisions that you get right, which leads to monumental success.

How many books does the average person read a year? The most consistent number reported was four. Whereas, the average CEO reads about 60 books per year. Millionaires read about 50 books per year. And billionaires are known for reading well above average. In short, reading leads to greater success. Greater success comes with better decision-making. Better decision-making comes from increased reading.

The most successful thinkers and thus often the greatest decision-makers in our society often cite reading as a major ingredient to their success. A few examples of those great decision-makers, just to name a few:

1. Bill Gates reads about a book a week.
2. Elon Musk was asked how he learned to build rockets. "I read books," he replied.
3. Warren Buffet said, "Read 500 pages every day. That's how knowledge works. It builds up, like compound interest. All of you can do it, but I guarantee not many of you will do it." (Blinkist Magazine, 2018).
4. Oprah Winfrey credits reading as being the major key to her success.
5. Mark Cuban reads three hours per day.
6. Mark Zuckerberg reads a book every two weeks.
7. Just to name a few past recent presidents who are known to have insatiable appetites for reading – George W. Bush, Bill Clinton and Barack Obama.

Roughly 70% of Americans do not read a full book after graduating from high school. The general unscientific rule is if you read three books in the same area, you will know more about that topic than most others. But if you read five books on the same topic, you are a subject matter expert to those not in that profession. (Rationality Lite, 2015) If you read five to ten books about the same topic, you are an expert, at least socially.

Leaders are readers. It does not matter if you are leading your family, a civic group of 4000, or a business of 40,000 people. You will be expected to make split-second decisions at some point, and your expertise will be relied upon and expected. The expertise that is within your power will be firmly steeped in your active reading habits.

It is critical that you consistently engage in directly focused reading goals in your profession, so that you will be more likely to make improved split-second decisions when it matters most.

Additionally, constantly reading books and maintaining productive activity of the brain has great benefits. For example, if you do not know anything about the subject matter that requires split-second decisions, you are much more prepared than the person who has not been reading. Why? As previously stated, reading increases your knowledge base and thus provides a larger pool of knowledge you have to draw from. It is all about the depth and wealth of knowledge that we can draw from when deciding. Please re-read if you compare a person who constantly reads books to the person who does not read. When faced with foreign split-second decisions, the person who has been reading has the advantage in likely making the more politically correct decision(s).

Nugget to share | There are additional lifetime benefits to reading. I have been practicing emergency medicine for over twenty years. I am fortunate to care and have cared for people from all walks of life and all age groups. But what I noticed early on in my career was that there was a plethora of older patients over the age of 70, who were just as sharp as the 30-year-old patients. And then there were those whose mentation was age-appropriate or were slow in their thought process and did not seem as mentally swift. Over the next ten to fifteen years, I started to do my own unofficial study.

The study was simple. I would ask patients over the age of 70 who I self-identified as "sharp" or not "sharp" what they thought kept them so "sharp or quick-thinking and witty." Sharp or quick-thinking and witty" simply means that based on their circumstances, they are swift and insightful in their thinking. I know you want to know more about the criteria, but there really is not more.

Most of those that were "sharp" knew why they were "sharp." They would say things like, "I read all the time," or "when I retired, I started reading more to keep my mind sharp," or "reading made me feel young." The other common answers were: "I walk all the time," or "I work out all the time to keep my mind right," or "I walk on the stairs all the time."

Overwhelmingly, those who were mentally swift read and/or exercised consistently. But what was crystal clear was that reading was protective from the typical effect of declining mental dexterity. Yes, we can decline even while working. The point is active focused reading has immediate and long-term benefits.

Let me also add as it relates to older people. We are often taught that when we retire that we have to do things to keep our minds sharp. And this is true. But there are a few caveats. You have to do things that are at the same pre-retirement level functioning. Meaning, if you were a rocket scientist before retirement, then reading children's books to children will likely make you happy, but it is less likely to keep you sharp.

Let's use the brain muscle analogy again. Your brain is like a muscle. When you consistently work out, your muscles become bigger and have better circulation. You are stronger and more limber. And mentally, you probably feel better just being in shape. You are usually more confident. But once you stop using your muscles or significantly decrease exercising, your muscles decrease in size, and you are not as strong. What you do not use you lose. Your brain is the same way. If you stop reading and working out, what you do not use you lose. Your brain loses track and becomes less efficient. Reading is exercise for the brain. It helps keep the brain big, strong, and smart.

Your decisions are better when you have a habit of deliberate reading. The lens of how you view the world and thus your decisions have a direct correlation with your reading habits.

The point is reading prepares, positions, and protects you in your decision-making capacity and skills. It gives you a larger pool of mental resources to draw upon.

Commit to reading at least twelve to fifteen books a year. Or read at least 30 minutes every day.

2. PEOPLE

The people you surround yourself with will often be key to you, making the most optimal split-second decisions. Split-second decisions are often unannounced and occur at inconvenient times. And that unexpected time may expose troublesome truths. It may show that those around you are not equipped to advise you during your split-second decisions.

Remember that the name "split-second" decisions may be a misnomer. To recap, the time component of split-seconds does not necessarily mean seconds. It simply means that there is a time constraint. Hence, there will be those times that you have more than seconds and will have time to seek the input of those around you.

This is where the people you have selected to have around you is key. You do not need them to be your friend; you need them to possess a body of knowledge or a critical thinking skillset that you can tap into to assist you with your split-second decision. Often when the split-second decision conundrum presents itself, it will come like a thief in the night when you least expect it.

The individuals you have chosen to have around you before the crisis are your weapons. These are the leaders within your sphere that you must be able to utilize. Surrounding yourself with people that hold a large breadth of experiences gives you access to not only the knowledge that they have learned from their experiences but to their networks as well.

As it relates to the people and friends you associate with during the years, months, days, and hours leading up to your decisions, they have a conscious and unconscious role. The people you choose to spend your time with reflect who you are. It is proven that if your circle of friends is made up of successful millionaires, it is very likely that you are going to find yourself in the millionaire circle one day. Similarly, teenagers who hang with other teenagers who earn good grades raise everyone's likelihood in that circle of making good grades.

In that same regard, "Qui cum canibus concumbunt cum pulicibus surgent." Translation, "If you lie down with dogs, you get up with fleas." If your circle of friends is made up of individuals whose values are not consistent with yours, then their input, depth of thought, and the quality of their contribution that you need during your split-second decisions will not be consistent with your thought process. Thus, you will be no better off.

In short, the persons you choose to surround yourself with, including those who you hire, are the same ones you will likely turn to for input when you need to make split-second decisions. Be sure that they are the right ones you would want to advise you during this critical period.

Just as a side note, the people who you choose to have at your side at work are not there to be your best friends. The two main questions that you should ask yourself are: Do I trust them? Are they good critical thinkers? Meaning, do they have the experiences and mental & emotional dexterity needed to best advise me during critical times.

3. BLIND SPOTS

A blind spot is a cognitive predisposition that impacts your judgment and decisions in ways that you are unaware of. Blind spots are rooted in your past experiences that you are often not consciously aware of that influence your current perspective. This occurs both consciously and subconsciously.

I know this was just discussed, but my experiences have shown that most people underestimate the importance of blind spots. We have already discussed the academic aspect of blind spots, but in an attempt to make it stick concerning how our "innocent" blind spots can creep in at any moment, let me share. Follow me. I know where I am going:

I was sitting down, completing the medical record of a patient I had just finished evaluating. Out of the corner of my eye, I could see an emergency medical service (EMS) crew wheel a patient in on a stretcher, and the crew was quietly waiting for triage. It was typical for EMS to bring patients to the Emergency Department (ED). The crews usually all come in the same door and then wait for the triage nurse to come and evaluate the patient.

EMS crews bring all types of patients from different parts of the city. It is rather interesting that no matter your station in life, if you suddenly need medical help requiring emergency transportation, God brings all walks through the same portal. I could get a drug abuser without shoes, or I could get a diplomat who moments before was having dinner in a plush hotel; both will enter the ED through the same door.

On this particular visit, it was odd that the EMS crew entered the ED quieter and more somber than usual. I looked up, and one of the EMS crew members caught my eye. The crew member gave me the look that an experienced paramedic gives a physician when there is a patient who will probably need an additional eye at triage. I put my chart down, got up, and went over to triage where the patient was lying on the stretcher.

As I approached, I saw a woman of about fifty sitting on the stretcher. Based on a distant peripheral observational survey, she did not appear ill or in distress; she looked well-hydrated and seemingly comfortable. The paramedic stood next to the patient and said, "Doctor, do you want to see something interesting?" He pulled the sheets back and moved the patient's already unbuttoned blouse to the side. Once the paramedic moved the blanket, I could see that my initial assessment was inaccurate. This was a disheveled patient who did not appear to be homeless but was clearly unkempt. In fact, her attire was outdated and soiled with food and other stains.

The paramedic said, "Look." I looked and saw what appeared to be the rhythmic movement of the patient's breast. The color of the breast was slightly lighter than the rest of her body, but the single breast was moving in an organized, slow rhythmic manner that appeared to be separate from the rest of the body. I was not sure what I was seeing, so I went closer. To my God-fearing and frightful amazement, what I saw moving was the patient's entire breast completely infested with maggots. The movement I observed was maggots moving the flesh from under the skin. They had completely taken over her left breast and were causing her entire breast to move. This was the first time in my practice of medicine that I had to walk away to regain my composure.

We triaged the patient, admitted her to the hospital, and placed her in a room. I completed a medical history and physical exam. She was a nice woman. I would not say completely clear in her thinking, but definitely not out of touch with reality. After finishing my initial workup, I immediately consulted the surgery service. A few hours later, the patient was admitted to the surgery service.

I talked to the surgeon a few weeks after the admission, and he gave me more follow-up. As it turns out, she had been previously evaluated at a different local hospital for terminal breast cancer. The patient had refused surgery and was started on chemo, but said that the chemo made her extremely ill. She refused additional chemo treatments. She was discharged home soon after that. The surgeon said, "she wanted to use maggots, which we do not offer..."

We all have problems in life, different as they may be. We all have burdens to bear. But this case was one that humbled me in ways that defy description. One final point: maggots feed on dead tissue and actually help keep the tissue clean. The maggots were honestly helping to sustain the patient's life, and the patient knew this fact.

The point is, I was biased towards the patient. I had assumed that since she appeared homeless and was not speaking the king's English that she had a psychiatric condition and did not know what she was doing. I thought I knew more than her.

My blind spot was that I could only see modern medicine and thought that I knew what was best for the patient. I let my biases interfere with the patient's plan.

Understanding your "blind spots" and thus attempting to either improve or minimize the blind spots are crucial. You can improve your blind spots by having more robust experiences in areas surrounding your own biases. There is no set volume of new experiences but rather focused and purposeful pursuit of quality and variety of experiences that can aid in fixing current blind spots.

Another way to improve your blind spots is to question some of your assumptions and ask others to do the same. Challenge how well you think you know yourself. Based on that feedback, you can slowly adjust your own pre-misconceptions.

Finally, people grow from their experiences. Think back and review your past experiences and the assumptions that you have drawn. Re-think and re-assess them and change your conclusions as needed. Reframing your past experiences using the concepts of neuroplasticity is an effective tool.

4. MEDITATION

It is the practice of focusing your mind, thoughts, feelings, and emotions in the present moment. It helps to provide clearer thoughts. As a result of neuroplasticity, over time, meditation changes the brain. People use different techniques to practice meditation. Meditation is a practice that people use various techniques to do. A popular method is mindfulness.

Meditation allows you to build networks or lay new tracks of calmness. You are increasing the neuroplasticity of your brain. Hence, when there is a sudden urgent situation where you need to be calm and thinking clearly, there is already an easily accessible track or pathway.

Meditation actively creates new neuronal pathways similar to a new path created in the forest. When you first walk a route in the forest, there is no trail. The more you walk the same route, the sooner you will find that a defined, easily accessible pathway will develop. And in the end, you will have a permanent path that you can easily access, at any time no matter if it is day, night, snow, or rain.

You can't wait until the storm to build a hut. You have to prepare a quiet place in advance of the storm. You do this through meditation.

Before you stop reading and say, "I do not have time to meditate," we are only talking about ten minutes a day.

The first ten minutes of your day sets the tone for the rest of your day. Spending the first ten minutes of each day meditating and creating neuronal pathways of peace and quiet that you can access in times of stress and strain are key. I know this sounds fluffy, but it is outside of the scope of this book to highlight the studies and examples that support ten minutes of meditation per day.

In short, through meditation, you can create a pathway for any situation that you choose. If you're a CEO and you know certain decisions are going to come to you rapidly, you can start to create brain pathways that will give you immediate access to the information that you need. This would be similar to how emergency department teams are trained to deal with acutely ill or trauma patients. We rehearse these scenarios and algorithms countless times, and in doing so, we create an easily and rapidly accessible brain pathway. If we were to wait until the patients arrive to learn what to do, we would fumble throughout the entire code. As a result, our stress hormones would be so high when the patients arrived, combined with the distractions of not being comfortable, we would worsen the crisis. Meditation does the same thing that rehearsed algorithms can do – create easily accessible tracks.

Mediating in the morning is ideal. In fact, meditating in the morning and outside have the optimal benefit. The morning wind has something to share with you. It has something to help calm you. The morning wind and sun tend to make you feel better on some level. It is in this setting that optimal neuropathways are created.

5. EXERCISE

Regular exercise improves blood flow to the brain, improves cognitive function, and improves memory. The hormones released as a result of exercising soothes the brain as well.

Science has shown that exercise reduces inflammation in the brain, stimulates chemicals that increase neuronal and vascular growth and increases the overall health of the brain.

Exercise increases the dexterity of your brain. Exercises that increase your heart rate above 140 are known to greatly improve your cognitive function. Static exercises similar to weightlifting improves memory and executive function.

How much exercise? The literature is all over the place in terms of how much. After synthesizing the information, I would suggest a minimum of an hour, five to six times per week of exercise.

Practical Use:

In short, your ability to think, reason, and decide is only as good as the circle of friends that you keep as well as your experiences. Increase your circle of influence, and you will increase your experiences as well. In fact, if you work out with your new circle, then you are truly maximizing.

This is true as it relates to people who you hire as well. We will address those around you at work in a later section.

7

SIX KEY STEPS TO SPLIT SECOND DECISIONS

It was late. My daughter had been up several times during the night vomiting, and I stayed up with her. The alarm clock went off at 5 a.m., and I had to be at work at 7 a.m. I had only about an hour or two of sleep. I walked into the ER, and it was busy. After seeing a couple of patients, I knew something about me was not right. I was not on my game. I was tired.

I went and evaluated a patient in our urgent care (bumps, bruises, and minor car accident). Let's name him John. John was an 82-year-old man who had just been involved in what was described as a low-speed motor vehicle accident. John's daughter, one of the other passengers, was in the trauma bay being treated by the trauma team.

John was healthy, energetic, and smiling and wanted to be discharged before I could even examine him. After a brief history, I examined John. His physical exam was normal, except he had what we in medicine call a "seat belt sign." It is when a patient has bruising along the neck, chest, and abdomen – the areas where the seat belt usually rests. Often this is the result of sudden and significant deceleration and impact. The presence of a "seat belt sign" should have alerted me to the higher likelihood of internal injuries.

John's blood pressure was on the lower end of normal, but he said that his blood pressure, "sometimes runs a little low." I talked to John about observing him in the hospital for a few hours, but he really wanted to be discharged. However, in the end, he said, "Doctor, I will do whatever you recommend." John was up walking around, going back and forth to his daughter's trauma bay. He was eating and drinking. I decided to discharge John.

Twenty minutes after discharging John, we received a call from the parking lot that a man had passed out. It was John, and he looked blue. His blood pressure was low. We placed an ultrasound on him, and he had a ruptured spleen. The entire trauma team was activated, and John was taken to the operating room. John did well. He was discharged three days later.

In this case, all the information I needed was there to help me make the correct decision. I missed it. What is my point? I knew I was emotionally and physically exhausted when starting the shift and should have appropriately adjusted my clinical practice. I knew that taking deep breaths calms you and clears your brain, at least momentarily. I failed to take a breath and think slowly before I released John. And finally, while tired, I could tell that my adrenaline was increased, my heart rate was elevated, and thus, I should have adjusted. I should have been more conservative about my approach to each patient. I should have slowed down, sought input from colleagues, or at a minimum, admitted the patient for observation.

Application

Four steps to making the right split-second decisions:

1. **Emotional state**
2. **Control your breathing**
3. **Control your heart rate**
4. **Visualization**

Training Your Mind For Split-Second Decisions

1. Your Emotional State

What if you are an executive who has to do evaluations for your executive team. Let me guess. You think your evaluations are objective and unemotional. Let's use medical schools as our example. Medical schools have deans that are akin to the CEO of corporations. Deans hire and approve faculty and departmental leaders known as chairs. The chairs and their faculty exercise their clinical practice at a hospital that is contracted with the medical school. Hence, each clinical specialty has a chair that reports to the dean.

For instance, the emergency department has a chair who is the executive of the emergency department. The surgery department has a chair who is the executive of the surgery department. Similarly, the internal medicine department has a chair who would be equivalent to an executive in the business world. Pathology, radiology, pediatrics, and so on have the same setup. This would be the CEOs executive team in the business world.

Ok, it is time for you to do mid-year evaluations for your executive team or staff. You, as the dean, must evaluate your executive team in several areas, by increasing market share, elevating clinical activities, and through financial viability. And you must give an overall score from 1 – 10 (e.g. 1 is poor – 10 is outstanding). Historically, surgical departments provided the vast majority of the fiscal impact to both the hospitals and medical schools. The evaluations are semi-annual, and you are meant to provide a retrospective assessment based on the entire past six months. And yes, at times, based on the evaluation, performance improvement plans are needed.

In this example, you have two equal co-executives, the internal medicine chair, Dr. Sally, and the surgery department chair, Dr. John. Dr. Sally has been timely, contributes greatly to executive meetings and the overall financial viability of her department is strong and continues to improve. Dr. John, the surgery chair, on the other hand, is often late, marginally contributes during executive meetings, and the finances of his department have been significantly decreasing over the past six months. However, during the last board meeting a few days ago, Dr. John provided information and made comments that made him look like a rock star in front of the university's executive board. Who would you give the better evaluation to?

A better evaluation was given to Dr. John. Why? As humans, over 70% of our decisions are rooted in emotion. By the top three measures, Dr. Sally should have earned a better evaluation, but the emotional aspect led to the surgery chair receiving a better evaluation.

Most people base their decisions on either emotion or logic. This is true of doctors, lawyers, middle management, CEOs, firemen, everyone. But the majority of our decisions are emotional.

Let me explain further. In response to an external stimulus, the brain sends a hormone into the bloodstream. That hormone then creates a feeling. The feeling is then interpreted by the brain along the spectrum of positive or negative. Subsequently, the brain makes decisions based on the feeling that is generated from a positive or negative assessment.

You don't have to understand this grossly watered-down explanation. More succinctly stated, for the most part, the brain makes decisions based on emotions.

With that being said, it is imperative that we identify our emotional state and even change it if needed at the time of our split-second decisions. More specifically, we make decisions based on how something feels. Does it feel right to us?

The concern is, at times, our feelings about a particular matter have been hijacked or impacted by emotions, distant to the event that we are about to make a decision toward. For example, have you ever had a frustrating morning at home? It is your turn to take the kids to school, and they're constantly fussing at one another while getting ready for school. When it is time to go, they're not ready. It's the morning that you are chairing a big meeting, and your kids all of a sudden suffer memory loss. They can't find their school uniforms, they forget to eat breakfast or fail to let the dog out. Finally, you get the kids to the car 10 minutes later than you should have, and as you are pulling out of the neighborhood, your oldest child, who should have known better, says that she forgot something.

To make matters worse, your kids start fussing at each other again in the car. You finally lose your temper in the car, your emotions escalate, and you run down the list of all the stuff that they did wrong that morning. You are still in control but are yelling by now. You drop them off and show up for your meeting a few minutes late.

During your meeting, one of your direct reports is not prepared. You are less patient with him and become easily frustrated with others. Why? Because you are still emotionally escalated from the situation that happened with your kids that morning. Your team is now being impacted by your emotions from a remote emotional experience. Your executive team is now experiencing an extension of your rampage from this morning. You, as a leader, can empower yourself and others to keep their emotions from being commandeered.

It is important to understand that when you are aware of your emotions, you are able to exert absolute control of your reactions, especially those feelings that have triggers, and minimize the likelihood of your emotions being hijacked.

To paraphrase, Esther and Jerry Hicks in the book, "Ask and It is Given," your emotions are indicators of the vibrational content of your being, in every moment. And so, when you become aware of the feelings of your emotions, you can also be aware of your vibrational offering. Once you are aware of it, you will have full control of your own powerful point of attraction. With this knowledge, you can now guide your life experiences in any way you choose.

Your emotions are about your relationship with yourself. And since your emotions tell you everything that you would ever want or need to know about your relationship with your source, we often refer to your emotions as your "emotional guidance system" (p. 44).

As we just learned, if your day started with events that caused you to be angry, sad, or upset, then how you feel during that day or perhaps during the entire period is going to impact your decisions. And if you are unaware that your emotional state has been commandeered, your decisions can not be appropriately adjusted.

If you combine Book Two of Aristotle's *Rhetoric* and Darwin's *The Expression of the Emotions in Man and Animals*, and an article written in Forbes magazine in 2017, "Here Are The 27 Different Human Emotions," according to a study, we learn that the most common daily emotions are those that impact our decisions and result in the following mood(s):

1. Fatigue/Tiredness
2. Fear
3. Sadness
4. Happiness/Joy
5. Helplessness
6. Anger

Putting it all together is the ability to understand and recognize your emotional state in the moment, which gives you the power to adjust your decision-making and, more importantly, your split-second decision-making. But first, you must be able to recognize which of your moods are dominant at that moment. Is this the angry you? Fatigued you? Sad you? Helpless you?

Now, we all remember, "knock, knock, who is there?" from when we were kids, right? For those of you who do not know, the "knock, knock" reference. It's a game where a question-and-answer joke is asked and then followed by a pun. It goes like this: one person says, "Knock, knock." And the other person asks, "Who is there?" Then the first person gives a name or description. The other person then responds by asking, "Who?" And then the joke, pun or wisdom is shared. Let's lighten things up for a moment.

"Knock, knock."
"Who's there?"
"Duncan!"
"Duncan, who?"
"Duncan (don't count) your chickens before they hatch."
Or,
"Knock, knock."

"Who's there?"
"Opportunity."
"Opportunity, who?"
"Don't be silly. Opportunity doesn't knock twice!"
Or,
"Knock, knock."
"Who's there?"
"Cow."
"Cow says, who?"
"No, a cow says *moo!*" (Jokes4us.com)

Starting today, I want you to emotionally check in throughout the day by asking yourself, "Knock, knock," and then respond to yourself, "Who is there?" This will be your opportunity to think about your current emotional state. Why is this important? You want to be able to self-direct yourself to a habit of constantly asking yourself, "What is my dominant emotion at this moment?" Based on your response, you will know which emotion or feeling is present at that time and appropriately adjust as needed. By being able to assess your emotional state, you will have greater control of your emotional offering.

Before we begin our short discussion on the six dominant emotions, let's pay attention to the emotion fear. It is the most dangerous of them all. It does not matter if fear is real or imagined; it can be the most debilitating emotion of them all.

The reaction to perceived fear starts in the brain. The brain, through the release of hormones, adjusts for the appropriate response: either defense (fight) or run (flight). The fear response starts in the brain. Again, it is so important to highlight the operative word – *response*. It is how you perceive or how you see yourself as it relates to the situation or external stimuli that dictates your response. It is how you see yourself in the world that decides if you have a fear or not, because it is your response that starts the loop.

Back to the brain. The amygdala in our brain is responsible for the perception of emotion. It also helps regulate aggression. The amygdala is basically focused on how important or how much something stands out to us. A threat stimulus like a wild animal triggers a fear response generated from the amygdala. This activation then triggers the flight-or-fight response.

The fight-or-flight response is the most basic survival function known to man, meaning that when confronted with a threat, our brains are hard-wired to do one of two things: stay and fight, or run. This is also known as the acute stress response. It is our body's natural physiologic response to a perceived threat or harmful life event.

The fight-or-flight response causes the release of hormones—epinephrine, norepinephrine, and cortisol, among others. These chemicals are also known as sympathetic hormones and are released from the sympathetic nervous system. The sympathetic nervous system that all humans have is the same system that allows a deer to run from an oncoming predator and allows a lion to attack its prey. The chemicals released by this system cause an increase in heart rate, blood pressure, pupillary response, and a state of hyperarousal. Cortisol can also cloud judgment.

Succinctly, the brain becomes hyperalert, fast breathing, and dilated pupils. Your brain automatically changes the amount of flow to different parts of your body. For instance, blood flow to your muscles and heart increase because of the increased demand placed as a result of your flight-or-flight response. However, areas of the body that are not essential to the flight-or fight response experience a decrease in blood flow like your gastrointestinal tract or your kidneys. Your cortisol surges, and your memory may start to cloud.

The hyperalert part is important, as well. I would also add in hypersensitive. In the fearful emotional reactive state, your senses go unchecked may be too "hyper" or overactive. Normal stimuli that are not seen as threats are now seen as so. Your baseline lens for assessing situations is viewed through the lens of fear, which is most often an inferior position.

The six most common, frequent and dominant emotions that can impact split-second decisions are: Fear, Fatigue, Sadness, Happiness/Joy, Helplessness/Overwhelmed and Anger

1. Fear

If fear is the dominate emotion, then:

- You are more worried about avoiding loss than you are about potential gain.
- You tend to be overly cautious and take less risk – more uncertainty.
- You tend to be more emotional in the setting of catastrophic decisions.
- You tend to make short sided decisions.

(Chanel, 2009)

2. Fatigued/Tired

If you are fatigued or tired while making split-second decisions, then:

- Don't make any major decisions that you do not HAVE to make while fatigued.
- Seek more input from others you trust.
- Be more conservative about your decisions (people are often less inhibited when tired).

3. Sadness

If sadness is your leading emotion, then you will tend to:

- Be less patient as it relates to decisions regarding financial goals.
- Be more systematic in your thinking.
- Be more giving of resources.
- Have lower goals (Chanel, 2009).

4. Happiness/Joy

If happy/joyous you tend to:

- Want to explore and thus needs more information.
- Tend to be more trusting.
- Sometimes overestimates the likelihood of success (Khazan, 2016).

5. Helplessness or Overwhelmed

If you feel helpless or overwhelmed, then you often view the world through the eyes of pessimism and bleakness and tend to:

- Believe that they have very little impact.
- Take no risks.
- Expect poor outcomes.

(Nobrega, et. Al., 2016)
(Leykin, Robers, & Derubeis, 2011)
(Wakeman, 2010)

1. Anger

This arguably is the most dangerous emotion of them all. If you are angry, you tend to:

- Want to take aggressive actions.
- Want to be more dismissive of other people's opinions.
- Make riskier choices.
- Tend to be careless in your actions and decisions.

This single emotion can increase the likelihood of being committed to a failing plan.

Additionally, anger may cause those around you to be fearful of you, the person in charge, which means that those who are around you are aiding in the TLC decision framework you are operating in and thinking from a fear perspective. Simply put, your anger creates fear in those who are assisting you and thus impacts their decisions (Litvak, 2010, p. 288).

Addressing how to neutralize each of the aforementioned

emotions are outside the scope of this book. But simply being aware of the emotions and the possible impact provides therapeutic helpfulness when it comes to split-second decisions and implementing the TLC framework.

More generally, the longer the time interval from the external stimuli that lead to that particular dominant emotion, the less impact that particular emotion will have on the decision (Lerner, 2014). Specifically, as it relates to anger, studies suggest at least a ten-minute delay from the time of anger to the decision can completely neutralize the impact of the angry emotion (Sneezy & Imams, 2014).

Ask yourself, "Knock, Knock, who is there?" and appropriately adjust for that current emotional state.

Darwin Online: Expression of the emotions (Lee, 2017)

1. Control Your Breathing

Normal breathing usually occurs at a rate of twelve to fourteen breaths per minute. At this rate, healthy breathing occurs and allows for the appropriate exchange of the gases, oxygen and carbon dioxide. From a respiratory perspective, this helps maintain normal body homeostasis.

Hyperventilation is fast and deep breathing. A breathing rate above sixteen is abnormal and disrupts homeostasis. The faster and the longer that you hyperventilate, the graver the impact. Hyperventilation most notably makes you feel dizzy, stressed, faint, confused, lightheaded, and anxious, just to name a few.

In general, breathing too fast often makes us anxious, while slower breathing tends to have a calming effect on our emotions.

Breathing is an unconscious function, but we can consciously assume control and manage our own breathing rate and depth. Newer research shows that deep breathing can immediately impact your emotional center. In 1991, Jack Feldman, a professor at UCLA, identified a breathing complex in the brain known as the Pre-Botzinger Complex. It is a complex cell group that plays an important role in the regulation of respiratory rhythm.

As part of the research, Dr. Feldman eliminated this area of the brain in 175 rats. The discovery was remarkable. It showed, "it's a tie between breathing itself and changes in emotional state and arousal that we had never looked at before," said Feldman (Kozub, 2017). The study eventually led to the discovery that by consciously altering the rate and depth of our breathing, we can immediately change our emotional state and thus our response to the world.

Hence, we have all known that slow deep breaths often have a calming effect. But now we know that practicing and controlling our rate and depth of breathing pattern, allows us to instantaneously impact our emotional state.

While researchers have yet to develop optimal breathing patterns for instant access to your emotional center, it does not prevent you from practicing and through trial and error, learning how to access your emotional center.

An article written by Ana Gutter in Healthline about the top eight breathing techniques suggest the following as it relates to focused breathing:

"You can do this technique by sitting or lying down in a quiet, comfortable location. Then:

1. Notice how it feels when you inhale and exhale normally. Mentally scan your body. You might feel tension in your body that you never noticed.
2. Take a slow, deep breath through your nose.
3. Notice your belly and upper body expanding.
4. Exhale in whatever way is most comfortable for you, sighing if you wish.
5. Do this for several minutes, paying attention to the rise and fall of your belly.
6. Choose a word to focus on and vocalize during your exhale. Words like "safe" and "calm" can be effective.
7. Imagine your inhale washing over you like a gentle wave.
8. Imagine your exhale carrying negative and upsetting thoughts and energy away from you.

9. When you get distracted, gently bring your attention back to your breath and your words.

Focused breathing increases the flow of oxygen to the brain, thus allowing it to function optimally. This aids in more heighten focus on the split-second decisions that you must make. Additionally, the brain experiences a state of increased awareness.

In sum, it is yet another pathway of accessing our emotions and thus giving us greater control over how we respond to the world. Imagine the possibilities as it relates to our split-second decisions. This is another instrument in our toolbox that gives us another advantage to improved split-second decisions.

Control Your Heart Rate

As discussed earlier in chapter two, slight increases in your heart rate often improve your performance, and from the same complex mechanism, give you an extra burst of energy and focus. For instance, when you are participating in a competitive sport or speaking in public, the physiologic increase in heart rate is helpful.

However, if your heart rate goes beyond the optimal range of appropriate physiologic response, several disruptions begin to result in abnormal cognitive processing, restricted vision, aggressive behavior, and muscle stiffness, just to name a few.

The optimal heart rate for peak performance is about 110- 140 beats per minute. After 145, your ability to process information and think clearly starts to be compromised. And after a heart rate of 180, there is almost a cataclysmic collapse or break down in your ability to appropriately process information cognitively. Hence, at a heart rate above 180, your decision-making capacity is greatly diminished.

Scientists are aware that stressful situations are necessarily aversive, you feel uncomfortable, and you want to do anything you can to get out of the situation. But now we know that the basic body requirements, like heart rate, immediately impact our brain and our ability to make decisions, especially split-second decisions.

You can check your heart rate by checking your pulse. Your pulse is a direct reflection of your heart rate.

There are two ways that you can do this anyplace and simply:

1. To check your neck or carotid pulse, lightly place your index finger and third finger to the right or left of your windpipe or just below the jaw bone. You will be able to feel your pulse. It is important that you learn to check your pulse before an emergency.

2. To check the pulse at your wrist, place your index and third finger just below flexion point beneath your palm on the opposite wrist (on the side of your hand you would use to hold items). You should feel your radial pulse.

Count your pulse for ten seconds, then multiple it by six, and that is your estimated heart rate. For instance, if you are checking your radial pulse and you count twelve beats in ten seconds, then you multiply twelve beats by six, and it gives you a heart rate of 72 beats per minute. For additional information on how to check your pulse, visit https://www.health.harvard.edu/heart-health/want-to-check-your-heart-rate-heres-how.

If your heart rate is above 145 and not due to known specific medical reasons, you should slow it down immediately so that we can optimize our decision skills.

- Take a long deep breath and hold it for three seconds and then repeat two to three times.
- Splash cold water on your face.
- Valsalva maneuver – Take a deep breath, keep your mouth and nose closed and then push down as if you are having a bowel movement for three to five seconds and then repeat a few times if necessary.
- Share what is stressing you with someone else. Seek wise counsel. A problem shared is a problem "halved."
- Deploy any relaxing techniques you have previously used.

Once while working in the emergency department, a young-looking gentleman in his 30s, arrived to the ER in the car of a personal friend. The patient was dressed for a work environment. Let's name the patient George.

George was confused, and his skin color was blue in triage. This was a sign of poor blood circulation and poorly perfused organs.

We obtained a set of vitals at triage. His temperature was normal at 97.9, respiratory rate was elevated at 22, blood pressure was low at 96/51, and his heart rate was tachycardic or elevated at 190.

George looked extremely ill, and he was too distressed to tell us his medical history. We put him in the resuscitation room and began to place an IV and obtain labs right before placing him on a monitor. Once on the heart monitor, it showed that George's heart rate was higher than what we had originally thought. It was 198.

I ordered the appropriate medications. As a side note, we had just switched over to a new ER, and many systems, processes, and kinks had not been worked out, and the nurse responsible for retrieving the medication was new. So yes, there were inherent delays in getting the medicine.

I had a few options in terms of split-second decisions. I could just wait for the medicine and do nothing. I could use our cardiac electrical defibrillator that was already attached to him and electronically via a controlled electrical shock cardiovert George. This would have been very painful for George. Or while waiting, I could massage his carotid artery, which has been proven to slow heart rate in the appropriate clinical setting.

While simultaneously preparing to electrically cardiovert George and anticipating that the nurse would arrive with the medicine, I decided to attempt the carotid massage technique. His heart rate came down slightly right away. George's mentation improved as well. I was able to convince George to try the Valsalva technique.

The carotid massage technique is when you apply pressure to a part of the carotid artery that has cells that will send a signal to the brain to slow the heart down. The provider performs this when the person's neck is in the extended position while lying down. Turn the patient's head away from the side that is going to be massaged and then apply pressure with your thumb or index finger just underneath the jawbone.

Using both the carotid massage and the Valsalva maneuver, we converted George to a normal heartbeat, rhythm, and rate. We did not have to cardiovert George or use the IV medicine that I had ordered. George's heart rate came down to the 90s, and his breathing rate normalized to about fourteen.

Once George's mentation completely improved, he shared with us that he had a condition known as supraventricular tachycardia (super-fast heartbeat that is often controlled with medication). And he had not taken his medicine. But usually, when he missed his medicine and felt his heart starting to beat faster, George could slow it on his own. But this time, he was not able to.

George was discharged within hours of being treated in the emergency department. What is the point of this story? This is just a clear example of being able to control your own heart rate in an instant.

1. Visualization

While there are many definitions of visualization, the most simple and productive way to think about it is, actively picturing in your mind the desired outcome of something before it actually happens. The concept is known to be used in sports but can be applied to performance, split-second decisions, events, important tasks, and so on. Visualization allows you to see the future the way you want it through your mind.

Visualization is mental imagery. The imagery may be created from external stimuli or internally motivated.

Succinctly, it is the process of purposefully creating the images in your mind of your desired outcome. The regular practice of creating mental images and expected outcomes creates neural pathways. Simply focused thinking or imagining the desired action will create neural pathways in your brain. As a result of what we previously learned about neuroplasticity, the more that you practice visualizing, the better you will become.

In the book, the *Neurophysiological Foundations of Mental and Motor Imagery*, the authors report that through many academic studies, "... these data strongly support the existence of distinct neural mechanisms of expertise in motor imagery, as a function of the individual skill level and independently of the imagery type. Interestingly, the brain plasticity which occurs during learning of a motor skill is similar to that observed learning through mental practice..."

Guided visualization is purposely focusing a skill, thought process, or plan of action of performance in your mind for the unique purpose of preparing your mind to be successful when the circumstance arrives. Practicing or rehearsing in your mind at times is as good as actually doing it.

Several studies were done that looked at the muscle size of athletes in various sports who only practiced visualization for a period for that particular sport compared to athletes who *actually* practiced the particular sport. The stunning result found only slight differences in the muscle mass size in the two groups. Did regular focused visualization help maintain muscle mass too? The results, suggested that the answer would be yes, but a linear line was unable to be drawn because of other factors. But the point is, that if muscle mass can be maintained from just visualization, then imagine the possible benefits of being able to visualize in just the mind alone.

The practice of imagining is a form of mental training. While visualization has been studied for decades, it first gained notoriety during the 1980s, when the Russians stringently applied the concepts during the 1984 Olympics and appeared to excel. As a result, it was discovered that athletes who routinely visualized and practiced their desired outcome experienced greater results (Baumgartner, 2011).

Visual imagery is the cognitive process with eyes opened or closed that purposefully creates mental images of the desired outcomes. The input for the development of the mental images may come from many sources. For example, it can simply be the image of you making the right decisions, or how you are going to feel after you have made the right decisions, or the image of you performing or giving a speech. The main point is that you have practiced visualizing the desired outcome (Padilla, Creem-Regehr, Hegarty, & Stefanucci, 2018, p. 29).

In medicine, while we do not label it what it is, we visualize often. For instance, in the acute care setting, we often visualize certain situations and what our response should be and what the expected outcome should be.

For instance, psychiatric patients in the ER just happen to be one group that I have learned to purposefully practice visualization with. Most psychiatric patients are stable and in need of help. They do not mean anyone any harm. In fact, acutely psychotic mentally ill patients are more apt to hurt themselves than to hurt anyone else. However, there are also those psychiatric patients who can suddenly become extremely agitated, impulsive, and very aggressive.

Most emergency departments and especially larger emergency departments have a locked and secure section where psychiatric patients who present in the ED can be monitored while being evaluated. In other words, there are no quick ways in or out.

Then there are those patients who are in the psychiatric part of the ER because they are experiencing cognitive impairment as the result of acute intoxication. Often these patients arrive in police custody as a result of their impairment. The police, at times, know that it is due to an illegal substance. Until medically cleared by a physician, the emergency department is the best place to bring this category of patient. Also, there are times that the patient may be a "true psychiatric" patient who has taken an illegal substance.

The most common culprit of drugs that cause normal citizens to appear as acutely psychotic and aggressive is phencyclidine (i.e. PCP). It is a hallucinogen that is known to cause erratic and violent behavior. Often patients who are acutely intoxicated with PCP present similar to patients who are experiencing a non-illegal drug, chemically induced altered mental status. Again, I make this subtle distinction because, as I highlighted earlier, pure acutely psychotic psychiatric patients are more likely to hurt themselves versus others.

Over the years, I have been dubbed the, "psychiatric whisperer" by my colleagues. I could often calm most agitated patients with my voice and interaction. I was able to do this countless times. In fact, I would go against protocol and go into aggressive patients' room alone to calm them down. As a side note, it was not my desire to go in alone, but to go in with all the security/police with me was a heavier lift towards calming the patient. But I always made sure that I had easy access to the door.

Hence, I had to learn to visualize exactly what I would do under certain clinical situations. I had to mentally practice, because if things went wrong, they were going to go wrong fast. Calling the hospital police, placing the patient in restraints, and chemical sedation were all options. For example, once while working in a hospital in Baltimore, Maryland, I was called to a psychiatric patient's room. At this hospital, the emergency department had its own locked psychiatric suite that was away from the emergency department.

When I arrived at the patient's room, there were three big security guards, a nurse, and a tech, all standing outside of the patient's room. I walked into the room and the patient turned her mattress over. The bedside table had already been turned upside down and the room had clearly been trashed.

The nurse updated me and said that the patient, let's call her Martha, was just brought in by the police for "bizarre behavior." Martha was well known to the staff. The nurse, as per protocol, had requested that Martha change from her street clothes into a hospital gown. The nurse said that she went in to try to help Martha change, and the patient appeared to start to escalate in her behavior.

The nurses stepped out and called security. When security came into the room with the nurse to assist the patient, Martha became extremely agitated and aggressive and starting yelling, cursing, and throwing items off her food tray at the staff. The nurses and the security personnel backed out, as Martha proceeded to trash her room. That is when they called me.

I walked into the room with my white coat and a very soothing voice. Martha was on guard and was ready to be aggressive towards me. I simply asked her, "Who has been upsetting and bothering you to make you so scared?" She immediately sat on the mattress-less bed and began to cry. I sat next to her, and we talked through a few things, and Martha agreed to let me and the nurse help her get changed.

Martha was a young 30-something year old woman with a very muscular frame. She was about 5'5" and 210 pounds.

After we got Martha settled, I let her know that I would bring her another food tray and that I would be back to examine her shortly. I walked out of the room as Martha was sitting happily and calmly on the bed. I walked out, and the nurse tech and security guards all told me what a great job I had done because otherwise, "things could have gotten bad for her." That is just tough security talk. I said, "No problem," and proceeded to walk down the hall to let myself out of the locked door.

A second after I turned around and was basking in my "super ER doctor psych patient whisperer status," I heard commotion behind me, followed by someone yelling, "Doc! Watch out!" As I turned around, I saw this, 5'5", 210-pound patient barreling down the hall towards me with an extremely angry, mean, and violent look.

The way I saw it, at that moment, I had two options: turn and prepare to take the initial violent impact and be prepared for full combat or do what I had practiced and visualized in my mind many times, run! Seriously, I knew this day would come. But I always thought it was going to be a patient intoxicated with PCP or cocaine who would give a few clues that he or she was escalating.

And just like that, I was running down the hall. Luckily, security was able to restrain the patient before she got to me. We placed Martha in four-point restraints and chemically restrained her.

Why run instead of physically engaging the patients? There are no winners in that situation. I could get hurt, the patient could get hurt, the staff could get hurt, and then as the physician in charge, it would be viewed as a failure of my leadership for allowing the situation to escalate to the point where a nurse and/or doctor engaged in physical combat with a patient.

Fortunately, I had visualized many times what my reaction would be to a patient who suddenly became agitated and wanted to do harm to me.

The point is, focused and practice visualization gives you an advantage over situations that you know are coming. You can give an instinctive response that has been well thought out and practiced well before the situation. Additionally, visualization does not only prepare you for that situation but similar scenarios.

The medical world also does a more formalized version of visual imagery without calling it visualization. For instance, in the trauma setting, the ER/trauma team is often given advanced notice of the trauma that is being brought by EMS to the emergency department. Everyone is assigned a specific position on the patient's bedside. Every team member is made aware of potential injuries. Everyone is asked to be prepared in anticipation of the expected injures. By preparation, we mean visualizing what equipment you will need for the likely injuries and have it prepared and ready. The way to prepare is through mental imagery of doing the procedure or your skillset.

The imagery even goes so far as the location of the trauma center. For instance, if you are located next to a highway, you visualize the equipment that would be needed for blunt trauma as a result of deceleration injuries, also known as car accidents.

Visualization gives us the advantage of preparing our minds in advance for predictable situations while simultaneously priming our minds to be able to make split-second decisions.

Tying it further together, what we are talking about is an intersection of MUST mindsets of leaders and visualization. You can create images of you making the right split-second decision. The good part is, with a few minutes of daily visualization practice, it starts to become automatic. You will no longer have to react because, using visualization, you would have been trained.

Dr. Albert Foong, a clinical psychologist and writer for Urbanmonk.net, shares an amazing strategy. He succinctly presents a set of exercises that go in order of easy to difficult over some time. In Dr. Fong's techniques, she highly recommends not moving to the next one until you have mastered the previous one. Dr. Fong is, in essence, creating neural tracks. I highly recommend the following for improving visualization:

1st Exercise

Find a photograph and take your time to analyze it. Memorize every detail you can. Then simply close your eyes and try to recreate it in your mind. Bring in as much as you can: the colors, the birds in the sky, the freckles on the skin — whatever is there. Open your eyes to get more detail if you have to. Remember that this is not a test. Do it until you get good at it.

2nd Exercise

For the second exercise, we're going three-dimensional. This time, take up a small object, perhaps your pen or your keys. Again, analyze all the details and memorize it. Take your time.

Now, close your eyes, and see the object mentally. The challenge here is to start rotating it. See every detail but from all angles. If you feel comfortable, begin to bring in some surroundings. Place it on an imaginary table. Shine a few lights on it and imagine the shadows flickering.

3rd Exercise

This third exercise builds on the second and can be hard for some people, although others will find it very easy. This time, recreate your little object, but with your eyes open. See it in the real world, right in front of you. Again, move it around, rotate it, play with it. See how it interacts with the objects in front of you. Imagine it resting on your keyboard, casting a shadow on your mouse, or knocking over your coffee cup.

4th Exercise

This is where things start to get fun. This time, we're bringing *you* into the picture. Think of a pleasant location. I like to use my favorite beach. Now, imagine yourself in it. It's important to be in the scene, not just thinking of it.

Bring in your other senses, one by one. What can you hear? Are the leaves rustling? Are there people talking in the background? What about the sense of touch? Can you feel the sand you are standing on? What about smell? Can you imagine eating an ice-cream and feeling it slide down your throat?

Again, make sure that you are in the scene, not just thinking of it. Make this mental movie as strong and vibrant and detailed as you can.

5th Exercise

And in the final exercise, we're going to make things a bit livelier. Bring up the mental location from the previous exercise. Now, begin moving around, interacting with things. Pick up a rock. Sit on a bench. Run in the water. Roll around in the sand.

Then, bring in someone else. Perhaps you could bring in a lover, and then choreograph a dance with him or her. Or you could imagine a friend. Hold a conversation with him or her. Imagine them smiling as you tell them a joke. Now, imagine them slapping you on the shoulder playfully. What does that feel like?" (Litemind)

One final example of why practicing mental imagery is so important is provided by the 911 system. The 911 system was first implemented in the United States in 1968. It is to be used for emergencies, whereas the 411 system was established in 1930. It is a non-emergency system that is used mainly for directory assistance.

Malcolm Gladwell, in his book, *Blink*, highlights the importance of practicing visual imagery and thus training your brain how to respond during emergency conditions:

"...everyone should practice dialing 911...," because he has often heard too many situations where, in an emergency, people pick up the phone and cannot perform this most basic of functions. With their heart rate soaring and their motor coordination deteriorating, they dial

411 and not 911 because that's the only number they remember, or they forget to press "send" on their cell phone, or simply cannot pick out the individual numbers at all. "You must rehearse it" (Gladwell-Blink).

Another way of rehearsing it would be to practice visualizing. Go over doing it in your mind. It is very likely that when you do need 911 services that you could be in a situation where your heart is racing above the 180 mark previously discussed, and you may not be thinking clearly. Thus, practicing, rehearsing, or visualizing could save your life or the life of a loved one.

8

SPLIT-SECOND DECISIONS – AN EXTRA DOSE

It was a hot summer day, and I was working in a rural ER in Maryland. The day just felt good. But that was all about to change. We got a call on the EMS emergency radio. The paramedic started in a panicked voice, "We have a nine-year-old girl who was found at the bottom of the pool. She is unconscious. We are unable to intubate the patient (i.e. to place a tube down her mouth) there is too much fluid. We are three to five minutes away." I responded, "Put her on 100% oxygen, and we will see you when you get here."

I went to the other end of the ER to let the charge nurse, Leah, know what was coming in. Leah was a 60-year-old hard-nose and excellent nurse, who had been working in ERs for the past 40 years. By the time I got returned, the crew was already in the trauma bay and transferring the patient.

I walked in to the room to find a nine-year-old girl laying there listlessly, pigtails and all. Fluid was coming out of all her orifices. Let's name her Hannah. Guess what happened next? I froze! I was suddenly scared. I had never frozen or been fearful in the past. She was the first pediatric trauma patient I had treated since having my daughter. Leah nudged me and said, "You can think about your daughter later. Get going." I snapped out of it and ordered for an intubation set up right away. The tech started an IV on the left, while a second tech started an IV on the right.

I asked for the clerk to get the Children's Trauma Center on the line and to transfer the line to the trauma bay. She had already called and responded, "I am on hold waiting for the doctor now."

I attempted to intubate, but I couldn't see anything because of the fluid. The respiratory therapist turned the suction up so I could clear the fluid. I still couldn't see her cords to help guide the tube into her trachea so that I could breathe for her. Hannah's oxygen saturation started to fall from the 80s to the 70s (98 – 100 is normal). We tried to suction and then bag her to push air into her lungs. Another trauma team member got another suction catheter. One therapist held one catheter down her throat, while another team member held the second and I said, "Ready? Go!" We were able to suction a lot of fluid fast so that I could see the cords. Bam! I placed the tube.

The oxygen saturation only came up to the low 80s. But there was fluid coming out of the tube. One of the respiratory therapists shared that he had just read in a journal about "placing drowning patients on their stomach when trying to ventilate…" I had never heard of such a thing. I thought to myself, "how would it look if I did this new maneuver that is not the gold standard of care and the patient died?" Yet, I had Hannah in front of me, slowly dying.

At that moment, the clerk yelled, "The Children's Trauma Center doctor is on the phone!" But before I took the call, I agreed with the respiratory therapist and directed them to turn the patient over and lay her prone.

I went to the phone and told the Children's Trauma Center doctor the situation. He was a slow-talking, calm older physician. He immediately began to offer recommendations. The pediatric trauma doctor recommended different things: Increase the PEEP. NO CHANGE. Increase the oxygen. NO CHANGE. Turn the patient on her stomach. There was a series of back and forth that went on for ten minutes with the team trying everything, and while waiting for changes, the x-ray team would come and do their part.

Then the doctor asked if I was ready to transfer the patient. She was so unstable that I did not think Hannah would make it, but I said yes. He responded, "The helicopter will be there in two minutes." He had dispatched the helicopter while we were talking.

I went and re-evaluated the patient. Now her blood pressure was lower, and her saturations were 79 – 80%. She appeared to be getting worse. So, I changed my mind about transferring Hannah and asked the clerk to get the trauma doctor back on the phone. At the same time, I could hear the helicopter landing, and something inside of me said to go ahead and transfer this patient. Plus, I knew that I had maximized my medical knowledge as it related to Hannah's care.

The helicopter paramedics flew the nine-year-old to the pediatric trauma medical center, and the ER team received word that the patient was in critical condition but improving.

One of the doctors reminded me that drownings with unknown downtime, where the patient is found unconscious, have a 90% one-year mortality. On follow-up, Hannah was discharged from the hospital a month later, fully neurologically intact, and was expected to live a normal life.

Application:

1. **Your first decision is your best decision.**

Unless there is additional information presented, your first decision is likely to be the most optimal decision. Your subconscious knows information that your conscious does not know. The odds are that your first decision or first choice is the best choice. For reasons well beyond the scope of this book, your subconscious mind has insights and knowledge well before you do consciously.

Let's look at a study that was done in 1994, based on the model of research conducted by "Damasio" in 1994, also known as "Iowa Gambling Task." It is a test that is believed to assess and stimulate how we decide.

The basic purpose of the study was to determine the relationship between decision-making and prefrontal cortex of the brain and how our brain is trained subconsciously to go for the best possible option there is, even before we know it consciously.

When we discuss the prefrontal cortex, we are referring to the area of the brain that is particularly associated with decision-making. This area processes and orchestrates complex thoughts, behavior, and experiences. For instance, the pre-frontal cortex is pivotal in determining good and bad; better and best. The pre-frontal cortex is also vital in assessing the future consequences of current activities and the prediction of outcomes.

Let me give a more practical example. We have all seen intoxicated people who do silly things. We observe them using bad judgment and poorly assessing situations. In fact, a hallmark of an acutely intoxicated person is the loss of their ability to appropriately evaluate outcomes. This is due to the impact that alcohol has on their pre-frontal cortex.

Most of the information that is fed into the prefrontal cortex comes from our subconscious mind, which accounts for up to 85% of the decision-making processes. Our conscious mind only accounts for 5 to 10% in decisions and is associated with thinking and reasoning before a final decision. As a reminder, subconscious thoughts exist in your brain that impact your behavior, although you are not aware of the thoughts. The subconscious is continually being programmed through the constant accumulation of information by your surroundings, what you read, your experiences, etc. (Maszak).

Interestingly, more than 100 million pieces of data are stored in our brains. At any given instance, when we are about to decide, our subconscious mind processes the data that is stored, along with the emotions which are associated with any given situation in the form of negative or positive, at a rate of around 11 million bits per second. It is due to this that our subconscious mind predicts the decision 7-10 seconds before we actually take the decision through our conscious mind that is, at that time, working only at a rate of 40 bits per second.

Back to the Iowa Gambling Task experiment. The participants are given four decks of cards. Each of the cards will allow you to win a certain amount of money or lose a certain amount of money. The participants are told that the goal is to win as much money as possible. What they do not know is that certain decks are more favorable towards winning.

Participants have to choose one card at a time. Each time they choose a card, they know if it is a winning or losing card. Decks A and B yield $100. Decks C and D yield $50. But with each card that is chosen, there is a chance of receiving a penalty as well. For decks, A and B, there is a higher cost penalty, $300, while for decks C and D, the penalty is $100. In short, decks C and D are more advantageous and will result in the largest gains throughout the experiment.

Additionally, each participant was connected to a monitor that measured sweat production. Sweat comes from sweat glands. Sweat is most commonly generated in response to stress and temperature. In this experiment, the temperature of the room was kept constant and was not too hot.

On average, participants picked up a pattern and deduced which decks were more favorable by cards 40 to 50. All participants were definitive about which cards were favorable by card number 80.

This was when the experiment became more interesting. The participants' skin electrodes showed an increase in sweat production by card 10 whenever they thought about selecting cards from decks that would cause loss. An entire 70 cards earlier. This means that the participants subconsciously figured the pattern out long before the participants' conscious selves.

What does this have to do with you? In sum, our subconscious synthesizes more information and is aware of the results and impact sooner than our conscious self. An easier way of looking at this is when you are not sure how to decide. Your first decision or the first choice will likely be the optimal choice. Your subconscious has already been at work.

People tend to trust their conscious decision-making. We are comfortable with what we know. But especially under stress, studies have shown that our subconscious selves may be more reliable. Our unconscious self is not distracted by the here and now and the environment. The unconscious self can immediately draw on past experiences without having to explain to the conscious self.

Finally, it was concluded from the study that easily seen reasoning might not be enough to make advantageous decisions. The subconscious mind already starts the process of decision-making that synchronizes the emotional and autonomic responses of the nervous system manifested in the form of autonomic arousal causing increased sweat gland activity and excitement, or fear widely known as "goosebumps." People often feel "goosebumps" as a hunch before deciding on subject matters that there is an inherent degree of uncertainty. This is actually your subconscious leading you towards the final verdict.

These responses were obviously lacking in the patient's group because they were not able to generate those autonomic responses, which might have prevented them from selecting the disadvantageous cards.

There is not a rule, policy, or procedure that is inclusive of all possibilities. In fact, this is true even in training and preparation. There will be times that your current knowledge base and experiences are consciously insufficient, combined with the fact that you simply may have too many decisions to make. Hence, your first decision is likely the best, especially when no additional information has been added to the situation. You can call it your first decision, your gut, your hunch, or your God talking to you. The fact remains that it is very likely that your first decision will be the most optimal of them all.

1. Prepare for your next decision.

Split-second decisions are steeped in time constraints, lack of information, and critical consequences. But part of the split-second decision pathway is that no matter the outcome of your split-second decision, be prepared for your next decision.

There will be times where, based on the result or lack of expected desired outcome of the first decision that you made, you may have been wrong. Another way of saying this is, the decision did not render the results that you may have expected.

As discussed previously, there will be times that, based on all the available information, you made the right decision, but the results were not what you expected.

If your first split-second decision was wrong, there are a few things to consider:

1. This is going to seem too basic, but many fail to think about it. Is there a way to change the initial decision? If so, go back and make a different decision. There are times but not often that you get a "second bite at the apple." People fail to inquire to see if they can change their initial decision.
2. What is the next best decision given the new current circumstances? This is the sweet spot. Most of us do not consider what happens or how you feel when the first decision is wrong. How you feel at that moment is not as important as being prepared to make the next decision.

The most important part here is, do not be paralyzed by a wrong decision. This is not the time for self-pity or "should-a-would-a-could-a." Yes, you have to accept responsibility, but you still have to be ready and able to make the next decision.

Let's make a few leaps. If you are deciding when there is a limited amount of time, you do not have the time to gather all the information that you need, and there are critical consequences, then I would assume that you are in a position of leadership. You may be a CEO, executive, first responder, mother, chief, father, principal, clergy, entrepreneur, etc. You are someone who makes decisions that impact the lives of others.

Here is the truth of the matter. "The king eats alone." There are decisions that you are going to make that will not always be right. At times people will die, programs will be lost, jobs eliminated, games missed, money lost, and the list goes on. Yes, we all enjoy being liked. But leadership by its very nature dictates that you have to make decisions and live with the consequences. You may not be liked, at times you may even be hated, but that is why you should be prepared to eat alone. As Lady Macbeth stated in Act 3, Scene 2 of Macbeth,

> ...Why do you keep alone, of sorriest fancies your companions making. Using those thoughts which should indeed have died with them they think on? Things without all remedy should be without regard. What's done is done." In other words, once you have made a wrong decision, there is nothing you can do about it, you must not wallow. "What is done is done.

And if you made the wrong decision, it is important that you:

1. Stay energetic and excited. Your team will respond the way they see you.
2. Thank those around you for their help.
3. Remain, or at least appear, confident.

Here are a few comforting thoughts for you to keep in mind:

A. While many will disagree, it is suggested in John Zenger's book, *Extraordinary Leader*, "the team that makes the most mistakes wins." I would say the leader who makes the worst decisions wins overall. The more decisions you make, the more you are going to be wrong or right. We don't learn much from our wins. We learn and grow more from what the lessons and experiences of our inaccurate decisions have taught us. And if you are right about every decision, then you are either not making enough decisions, or you are making decisions that are so small that no one cares if they are right or wrong.

B. Most wrong decisions create problems, as the late Peter F. Drucker, 21st-century business management expert, wrote, "Most problems cannot be solved. Most problems can only be survived. And one survives problems by making them irrelevant because of success...

One focuses on success, especially on unexpected success, and runs with it." Succeed!

C. John Maxwell, in his book, *21 Irrefutable Laws of Leadership*, highlights that leaders are expected to sacrifice more than others. In fact, in the same book, Gerald Brooks, a leader says, "When you become a leader, you lose the right to think about yourself." You lose the right to feel sorry for yourself. You may have been wrong, but it is about the team. Get over it and prepare for your next decision.

More succinctly, no matter the outcome of your first split-second decision, the nature of split-second decisions means that you should be prepared to make the next decision.

Finally, there will be times that you truly made the wrong decision. Once the dust has settled, in the quiet, you will discover a lesson or lessons learned from the entire situation. As many of us have learned, leadership is not for the faint of heart, but there are wrong decisions that will lead to what others call failures.

Lessons are required for success. The lessons and the gold come from the difficult "losses" and experiences you have learned in life.

The late American poet, Douglas Malloch, best known for his work, "Be the Best of Whatever You Are" in one of his less well-known poems, "Good Timber Does Not Grow on Ease," concisely characterizes the lessons needed to be great:

> *The tree that never had to fight*
> *For sun and sky and air and light,*
> *But stood out in the open plain*
> *And always got its share of rain,*
> *Never became a forest king*
> *But lived and died a scrubby thing.*
> *The man who never had to toil*
> *To gain and farm his patch of soil,*
> *Who never had to win his share*

Of sun and sky and light and air,
Never became a manly man
But lived and died as he began.
Good timber does not grow with ease:
The stronger wind, the stronger trees;
The further sky, the greater length;
The more the storm, the more the strength.
By sun and cold, by rain and snow,
In trees and men good timbers grow.....

In summary, you have to go through a few wrong decisions to become a better leader and then finally, a great leader.

1. Do what feels right or do what is kind.

We do not make decisions in a vacuum. As we have learned, there are many variables and a great deal of information to consider. Perhaps too much. The very nature of split-second decisions says that we do not have an adequate amount of time and or information to help maximize our decisions. Humans tend to place different weights on pieces of information. In an article appearing in Kellogg Insight, the authors write the following:

"Norgren and his colleagues caution against a one-size-fits-all strategy toward decision-making. Conscious decision-making certainly has its advantages and is not without its place. Math, for example, cannot be performed without paying close attention, because consciousness goes hand in hand with precise, rule-based thinking. Thus, humankind's stunning advances in fields like science and engineering depend on healthy doses of conscious calculation. However, the researchers' results indicate that consciousness has limited capacity, and only a fraction of the relevant information can be considered for very complex decisions. Moreover, conscious deliberation has been shown to inflate the importance of certain features at the expense of others, distorting the outcomes."

Explained by Norgren, "Conscious thought is like a spotlight on a

Training Your Mind For Split-Second Decisions

decision. It illuminates very brightly, but only a particular, narrow aspect of the problem. It has very limited processing capacity. Unconscious thought, on the other hand, is more like a child's night light, casting a dim light on the entire decision space without focusing in on any one particular thing." (Kellogg Insight)

There will be times when you really need more time or information. There will be times where the consequences are severe for you or someone else. There will be times when your analytics and theories fail you. There will be times where those around you, confuse you with their input. And there will be those times where what you think is the right thing is different from what the current data and evidence suggest. Or you know the best decision, but it is not aligned with the organization's policies, procedures, and culture. There are times where you have to do the "right" thing. There is nothing dramatic and or deep about doing the "right" thing.

For the sake of staying focused, we are not going to define the "right" thing. It is the thing that feels right. It is the gut feeling that says this is "right." It is that thing when even if the "right" thing turns out wrong, you can still feel good about your decision.

At the end of the day, you may truly not know what to do. When there is no additional information available to you at that time that will help, it is best to lean on doing what is kind and feels right.

For example, I was working the evening shift in an ED in the Midwest. It was a typical, busy Monday. There were several acutely ill patients: one with chest pain who was having an acute myocardial infarction, also known as a heart attack. There was a patient who had diabetic ketoacidosis (i.e. blood developing acid secondary to uncontrolled diabetes) and a septic patient (i.e. an infection that has spilled in the patient's blood) from a severe urinary tract infection who needed to be admitted to the intensive care unit. There were a few intoxicated patients, and then there were the run of the mill headaches, sore throats, I-am-feeling-depressed-because-my-boyfriend-broke-up-with-me, abdominal pains with nausea and vomiting, and homeless patients who were waiting for the bus to the shelter. For those of us in the business of emergency medicine, this was considered a very busy day.

There was an alcoholic patient whom we'll call Mr. Jack. He was acutely intoxicated. Mr. Jack kept getting off of his stretcher and attempting to wander into other patient's rooms. We finally had to restrain Mr. Jack.

In many emergency departments, there are what we call local alcoholics, meaning they have been to our ED several times for the same reason, acute intoxication. The staff gets to know these intoxicated patients very well and even develops a clinical gestalt for what their alcoholic patterns are going to be for each visit. For example, there is Mr. Smith, who we all know is going to come into the ED unashamedly drunk, loud and unruly. No, we don't need to call security to restrain him. We know that if you give Mr. Smith a sandwich, apple juice, put the sheet over his head, and make sure that his feet are covered, he will be very quiet and cooperative for the rest of his stay. Mr. Smith will wake up sober, thankful, and very pleasant. He is our "local alcoholic." By the way, Mr. Smith still receives all the other appropriate treatments needed for each visit.

Mr. Jack, on the other hand, was new to the ER. We had never seen him before. He was my patient. I had gone over to his stretcher several times, asking him to lie down. He would lie down for about 15 minutes and then get back up. I ordered a mild sedative, and this calmed him for about twenty minutes. As I was coming out of another patient's room, I noticed that Mr. Jack was off his stretcher and had wandered to the other end of the ED. I went over to Mr. Jack and asked him to please lay back down, and that I would give him additional medicine to help him relax. While Jack was waiting to receive the additional medicine, he physically assaulted a staff member.

Jack was a fit, stocky, 5'10" 40s-something male. Jack's aggressive behavior escalated even more after the assault. As per protocol, the police were called. Jack was arrested. A few days later, the person who had been assaulted was posturing to file a lawsuit, because he thought that the hospital should have done a better job of protecting him from Jack.

As a result of the assault, the hospital administration reacted with sweeping policy changes as related to staff and patient safety.

A few days after the rule changes, Mr. Smith came in hungry and acutely intoxicated. We were supposed to restrain him. Somehow the police were called, and they were at the front desk putting their gloves on, ready for action. We knew that Mr. Smith would fight with the police.

There were new policies and procedures, and Mr. Smith was standing in front of us in his typical agitated state. With the policy and procedures, representatives were ready to leap into action, and they swiftly moved in our direction.

We had to either follow the policy and procedures or let Mr. Smith be exposed to the likely violent interaction with the police. We chose to do the right thing. We asked the police officers to stand down, and we gave Mr. Smith a sandwich, apple juice, put the blanket over his head, and put him in the back hallway.

1. **All you can do, is all you can do. Decide!**

As long as you have done what is required to make the best decision, then you have done all you can do. Meaning you have:

- Checked and adjusted for your emotional state, you have consulted the available right people for that circumstance, and you have applied the TLC framework.

Notice, I did not say as long as you have done your best. You do not know what your best is. You can always better your best, which means our best is never our best. You have to do all you can do. As Les Brown said, "All you can do is enough. As long as you have done all you can do." Do what is required.

1. **Choose your team wisely.**

Let's call the split-second decision the arena. In the simplest form, anyone around you, when you have to make a split-second decision, is in your arena. A real-life example of this is the trauma/resuscitation bay in the emergency department. It is the arena. The vast majority of split-second decisions in the emergency department are made in the trauma/resuscitation arena. In the arena of the emergency department, we, with great diligence and purpose, control the people who are allowed in the arena while split-second decisions are being made. Meaning, the clerk is an important member of the team not allowed in the arena. The radiologist or dermatologist, who is a physician, is not allowed in the trauma arena. Yes, they are doctors, but the input they would provide would be a distraction and very likely a waste of valuable time. We purposely surround the physician and nurses with people who can help provide immediate answers about acute resuscitations in the trauma arena so that split-second decisions can be made.

Actually, we understand so seriously how the people around you impact your decisions and that those who are allowed in the trauma resuscitation arena have assigned places to stand. There is one leader.

They are the ones who you will turn to for help. The final decision may be yours, but until that final decision is required, you can seek as much information from anyone or anything. If it is work-related, those who surround you at work will likely have the greatest impact. Yes, I get that you may not get to choose those who you surround yourself with at work. But you get to choose to get to know them well enough, that intuitively you know who and what you can rely on them for and in what circumstances as it relates to information and advice.

Those you surround yourself with outside of work are typically people you choose to have in your world. They reflect you. Hence, you have to know your flock. You should know who you can seek advice and reasonable council from in various situations. For instance, you should know who to turn to when things are difficult and you need clear and concise input. The quality of the input they

Training Your Mind For Split-Second Decisions

give is only as good as the quality of the person. You must associate yourself with only qualified people.

You always reserve the right to reach over in either group and seek input. But just know in most split-second decisions those most proximate to you are going to have a greater impact.

More practically, as people, sometimes we can't control who is around when the split-second decision conundrum arises. There may be times when you may need to ask certain people to step out of the room. If they can't help with the decision, then they can hurt by being a distraction. Sometimes they are the people who may have helpful information, but the negative energy or stress they bring to the arena may not good.

9

PREPARE TO BATTLE YOUR DEMON – THE WAR

There is a war going on every day. You are expected to be more than a soldier. You must be a warrior, a warrior who is willing to win at all costs. A warrior acknowledges fear and moves right past it as if it did not exist.

The war you are in is the toughest one you will ever be in. In this war, you do not have a gun. And the enemy has a strategic advantage. Why? Because you're in a battle of your mind, and your mind knows your fears. It knows your deep, dark lies, and it starts and will use them against you. Your mind wants to push you in a direction that is comfortable and easy, the route that does not involve rigorous mental training. Your mind wants to naturally take the less difficult route. The route that does not involve training.

Your opponent knows and likes comfort, does not want to change, and does not want the stress of being wrong. He or she knows your every move. It is a battle of the self that wants it easy and avoids discomfort versus the battle of the self who sees on the other side of fear, training, and hard work. It seems that by training your mind to make split-second decisions and working past your obstacles is greatness.

Everybody wants the quick and easy way. For instance, how to achieve the perfect body in ten days, or five quick exercises to instantly improve your memory. Those are gimmicks and sales. True change and turn around requires hard work and pain. And there is a gift in going through the pain of growth. A better you. An improved mindset and a better leader.

Yes, as you go to battle with your mind over who controls the territory of your mind, you will lose a few battles. But in the losses of those battles are the best lessons of life. It will be difficult, and it will be hard, but if you do what is hard now, your life will be easier later.

Application:

Let there be no doubt that split-second decisions are all calculations. They are based on many factors in your conscious and subconscious mind. Making split-second decisions is not an overnight process. Notice that I have taught you how to, through hard work, optimize your split-second decisions. And as you can see, the process takes time to maximize. I did not teach you how to make quick decisions overnight. It is a process. You have to change your brain and your mindset to improve your split-second decisions. Most importantly, you have to win the battle in your mind.

Principle 1:

1. The first thing you must convince your mind of is that losing is not an option. And then you have to nurture your mind to thinking, "I will never lose again."
2. Quitting is not an option. Your mind is going to want to do what is comfortable and what is simple. Training your mind to make split-second decisions is doable. Convincing your mind to do the hard work so that you are ready when the split-second time comes is the difficult part. It's still doable, as long as you win the war.
3. You need to convince yourself that it is a process. The more you commit to the process of improving your split-

second decisions, the faster the progression will occur. It is not a gimmick. It is not three steps to a perfect body overnight. It is about improving your life.

4. Minimize fear. I am going to purposely dumb this down. After all, there are thousands of books written about fear, but the details are outside the scope of this book. More poignantly, as it relates to your fear, do not deny it. Most people struggle because they want to deny their fears. But what is clear is simply acknowledging your fear and then deciding to move past fear is efficient and empowering.

Principle 2:

Your mind must be willing to fail. Yes, fail! A more accurate way of stating it is: you must be willing to learn lessons. If you are not willing to fail, you are always worried about failing and therefore do not completely unleash your full potential.

I completely understand. It is painful to give something your all and not achieve the measurable goal you had planned. As a result, you give it what you think is a respectable effort. And if you do not succeed, you can always hide behind, "I did not do my best." Hence, you are constantly holding back because you are scared to fail.

Or you say, "I gave it my best." How do you know what your best is? Let's look at the world of sports, long distant running. Since the inception of time, it was always believed that the four-minute mile could never be achieved. Thousands of runners attempted the four-minute mile and would not attain it and then defaulted to, "I gave it my best."

Then on May 4th, 1954, Roger Banister of Oxford, England broke the four-minute mile record. But it is what happened soon after that, that is really interesting. After Roger became the first officially documented human in history to conquer what had eluded countless, several more people in that same year broke the four-minute mile.

The point is you do not know what your best is. You can always better your best. You can't allow your own self-imposed fears and limitations to become the obstacle that prevents you from achieving your true potential.

I can teach you these, but until you actually go out and make split-second decisions, then you are just practicing. You beat your mind by practicing what you are trying to improve. You have to practice what makes you uncomfortable. The changes you need to make to significantly improve your split-second decisions will require you to battle your mind. And you must win.

CONCLUSION

We will all be faced with decisions that will change the trajectory of the lives of those we lead. Most of those life-changing and life-altering decisions will be split-second decisions. We are not talking about quick decisions or decisions that you make under pressure but decisions that have critical and serious consequences. And of those 35,000 decisions that we make every day, if we simply learn and train to improve less than 1% of those decisions, we will have epic and massive success in not only our businesses but in our personal lives as well.

Learning is not enough. You need to train. In life-altering split-second decisions, you have either been trained, or you are guessing. If you are a leader, it is the same for your employees. They have either been trained, or they are guessing.

As leaders, we want to create an environment that is primed for those steeped in it to be successful. Train your leaders to make optimal split-second decisions. The more trained you are for split-second decisions and other emergencies, the better the quality of those decisions.

The truth is you never know when or how many split-second decisions you will have to make. But you must be able to recognize

Training Your Mind For Split-Second Decisions

when you are in a split-second decision scenario and be prepared to use your training. For example, I was working in a hospital that had a mixture of insured and uninsured patients. The area was known to have an increasing drug problem. It was the flu season, so the ER was busy. Frankly, our resources were overwhelmed. The wait time to be seen by a doctor for non-life-threatening emergencies was over eight hours.

In an attempt to evaluate non-urgent patients faster and free up space in the ER, executive leadership decided to put all urgent patients in one closed area near the rooms that they would be evaluated in. The downside of the waiting area that we moved them to was that they all would be in very close proximity to each other.

I was the physician leader, but I had three or four highly qualified and experienced nurses and techs. We were moving patients swiftly. "Treat them and street them" is the phrase we use when we are moving patients efficiently in the ER. And that is exactly what the team was providing, high quality and highly efficient care.

While I was in between patients, I looked into the waiting area, and to my surprise, I observed patients who had been waiting for a while, talking to the people next to them. They were just sharing their individual life stories.

The next patient I treated was a 70-year-old friendly lady, who was well dressed in red shoes, to match her red outfit. While treating the patient, she said, "I live alone and have to go catch the number four bus to get home. From the bus stop, I have to walk home alone. Once I get home, I have to go into a dark home because I live alone." The tech, nurse, and I all looked at each other and laughed. I said, "In other words, ma'am, are you asking us to hurry up?" We were more than happy to expedite her care. In fact, we gave the patient her first dose of medicine so that she would not have to have the prescription that I wrote, filled until the next day. She was treated, released, and was happy.

We called the next patient. He was a friendly, cool, chatty young 30-year-old male. The patient said, "I need Percocet. I hurt my back while lifting boxes at work and need some Percocet." Percocet is a potent narcotic in the same class as heroin and fentanyl. I told the young man that I would examine him, but it was unlikely that I was going to give him Percocet. I also added that anti-inflammatories like Motrin are best for back pain.

I briefly examined him, and his exam did not suggest the need for a narcotic.

I went on to explain to the patient my findings and that I was going to discharge him with Motrin. The patient's mood changed. He became really cool, calm, and confident. The patient said, "You are going to give me Percocet one way or the other." The nurse and tech looked at me in a shocked bewildered look. I responded and said, "We will not be ordering you Percocet, and we will be discharging you."

The patient then shocked all of us. He leaned back and crossed his leg, and confidently said, "We can do it your way, or we can do it my way. You remember the old lady in the nice dress with the red shoes, who is going to go catch the number four bus who lives alone that you just saw?" My mind flashed back. I remembered seeing the two talking, while they were in the small waiting area. The nurse, tech, and I all had a shocked look on our face. I said, "Yes, I remember her." The young man then went on matter-of-factly to say, "You can either give me my Percocet or I am going to go knock that lady upside her head and get the money I need for my stuff" (i.e. Stuff means illegal drugs).

I reexamined him, and as it turned out, the young man needed a prescription for Motrin *and* Percocet. I went and evaluated a few more patients, while I was preparing his discharge papers. By the time I discharged the young man, I was sure that the lady was home safely.

Many split-second decisions needed to be made. This was a crisis. There may not have been several lives at stake in this particular scenario. Nevertheless, it was a crisis for the patient and those involved in her care. For instance, the nurse involved in her care had to make the split-second decision to go against the doctor's recommendation and call the administrator on call. The tech wanted to make the split-second decision to call the police. And then, as the leader, there were numerous split-second decisions that I had to make about the entire scenario.

While there, I had not received specific training on how to deal with a person wanting drugs who threatened to hurt a patient recently treated, but I did have training on how to make split-second decisions.

What is my point? You must have a framework for how to make sudden decisions when you may not have all the information and there are critical consequences. In this case, the nurse got the head nurse, on-call administrative folks, and others on the leadership team. There will be many crisis that require split-second decisions that impact an end-user and your leadership team. And as a leader, how you manage each crisis will impact your ability to lead those around you. You must have a framework for making the many split-second decisions that you will have to make daily.

I hope that this book and the lessons that have been taught have equipped you with the tools needed to help you and your organization grow and have epic success. For most businesses, the only factor separating it from massive growth and success are split-second decisions.

Finally, you are not God or whoever you view as your God. Therefore, you should know that there will be times that you will be wrong. The rules and lessons learned in this book have equipped you with the TLC framework and most of the rules for making your decisions and especially your split-second decisions. The TLC Framework is the ideal framework. It works in almost every situation. The TLC framework trains good leaders to make great split-second decisions.

REFERENCES

Baer, D. (2014, Dec. 2). Always Wear the Same Suit: Obama's Presidential Productivity Secrets. *Fast Company*, Work Smart. Retrieved from https://www.fastcompany.com/3026265/always-wear-the-same-suit-obamas-presidential-productivity-secrets

Baer, D. (2015, Apr. 28). The Scientific Reason Why Barack Obama and Mark Zuckerberg Wear the Same Outfit Every Day. *Business Insider*. Retrieved from https://www.businessinsider.com/barack-obama-mark-zuckerberg-wear-the-same-outfit-2015-4

Baer, D. (2013, May 14). Quick: End Decision Fatigue Before It Drains Your Productivity Reservoir. *Fast Company*, Leadership Now. Retrieved from https://www.fastcompany.com/3009641/quick-end-decision-fatigue-before-it-drains-your-productivity-reservoir

Baumgartner, J. (2011). Visualize It. *Psychology Today*. Retrieved from https://www.psychologytoday.com/us/blog/the-psychology-dress/201111/visualize-it

Chanel, O. et. Al. (2009). The Influence of Fear in Decisions: Experimental Evidence. *Journal of Risk and Uncertainty*, vol. 39(3). Retrieved from https://chichilnisky.com/pdfs/Chanel_Chichilnisky_Influence_of_fear_in_decision_Definitive%20FINAL.pdf

References

Daniels, T. (2015, Nov. 15). What are Some of the Greatest Examples of the Subconscious Mind? *Quora*. Retrieved from https://www.quora.com/What-are-some-of-the-greatest-examples-of-the-subconscious-mind

Eli, Inc. (2016, Mar. 31). Five Real-World Examples of Unconscious Bias. ELI Inc. Retrieved from https://www.eliinc.com/five-real-world-examples-of-unconscious-bias/

Hicks, E & J. (2004). *Ask and it is Given*. Carlsbad, California. Hay House, Inc.

Holmes, C. (2007). *The Ultimate Sales Machine: Turbocharge Your Business with Relentless Focus on 12 Key Strategies*. New York, New York: Penguin Group.

https://en.wikipedia.org/wiki/Rhetoric_(Aristotle)

Jokes4us.com. Retrieved from http://www.jokes4us.com/knockknockjokes/knockknockbusinessjokes.html

Jokes4us.com Retrieved from http://www.jokes4us.com/knockknockjokes/knockknockbusinessjokes.html

King, C. M. (2018, Apr. 20). Bill Gates Reads 50 Books a Year – Find Out Why. *Blinkist Magazine*. Retrieved from https://www.blinkist.com/magazine/posts/most-ceos-read-60-books-per-year

KelloggInsight. (2009) Too Conscious to Decide? Retrieved from https://insight.kellogg.northwestern.edu/article/too_conscious_to_decide

Khazan, O. (2016, Sept. 19). The Best Headspace for Making Decisions. *The Atlantic*, Science. Retrieved from https://www.theatlantic.com/science/archive/2016/09/the-best-headspace-for-making-decisions/500423/

Kozub, S. (2017) Take a Deep Breath – No Really, it will Calm Your Brain. *The Verge*. Retrieved from https://www.theverge.com/2017/3/30/15109762/deep-breath-study-breathing-affects-brain-neurons-emotional-state

Krockow, E. M. (2018). How Many Decisions Do We Make Each Day? *Psychology Today*. Retrieved from https://www.psychologytoday.com/us/blog/stretching-theory/201809/how-many-decisions-do-we-make-each-day

References

Lee, B. Y. (2017, Sept. 9). Here are the 27 Different Human Emotions, According to a Study. Forbes. Retrieved from https://www.forbes.com/sites/brucelee/2017/09/09/here-are-the-27-different-human-emotions-according-to-a-study/#7d4de8721335

Lerner, J. (2014). Emotions and Decision-Making. *Annual Review of Psychology*. Retrieved from https://scholar.harvard.edu/files/jenniferlerner/files/annual_review_manuscript_june_16_final.final_.pdf

Leykin, Y., Roberts, C. S., & Derubeis, R. J. (2011). Decision-Making and Depressive Symptomatology. *Cognitive therapy and research*, 35(4), 333–341. https://doi.org/10.1007/s10608-010-9308-0

Litemind. Retrieved from https://litemind.com/how-to-develop-visualization-skill/

Litvak, et. Al. (2010). *Fuel in the Fire: How Anger Impacts Judgement and Decision-Making*. Retrieved from scholar.harvard.edu

Maszak, M. S. *Mysteries of the Mind*. Retrieved from http://webhome.auburn.edu/~mitrege/ENGL2210/USNWR-mind.html

Montagne, R. (2016, Oct. 17). How the Concept of Implicit Bias Came Into Being. *NPR*. Retrieved from https://www.npr.org/2016/10/17/498219482/how-the-concept-of-implicit-bias-came-into-being

Nobrega, J. et. Al. (2016, Nov. 18). Strong Interactions Between Learned Helplessness and Risky Decision-Making in a rat Gambling Model. Scientific Reports (6). Retrieved from https://www.nature.com/articles/srep37304

NYU Langone Medical Center. (2014, July 17). Measuring nurture: Study shows how 'good mothering' hardwires infant brain. *Science-Daily*. Retrieved from www.sciencedaily.com/releases/2014/07/140717094554.htm

Padilla, L. M., Creem-Regehr, S. H., Hegarty, M., & Stefanucci, J. K. (2018). Decision-making with visualizations: a cognitive framework across disciplines. *Cognitive research: principles and implications*, 3, 29. https://doi.org/10.1186/s41235-018-0120-9

Parce, J. (2015, Mar. 10). Read 3 Books to Know More About a Topic Than 95% of People. *Rationality Lite*. Retrieved from https://medium.

com/rationality-lite/read-3-books-to-know-more-about-a-topic-than-90-of-people-5fea803bf533

Sneezy, U & Imams, A. (2014) Mataarazzo Effect and the Strategic use of Anger in Competitive Interactions. *Proceedings of the National Academy of Sciences Advance Online Publication.*

Wakeman, C. (2010, Oct. 12). Why Learned Helplessness is the Fast Track to Disaster. Forbes. Retrieved from https://www.forbes.com/sites/cywakeman/2010/10/12/why-learned-helplessness-is-the-fast-track-to-disaster/#4b2896df1af8

Weiss, D. C. (2011, Aug. 22). Study of Israeli Parole Board Shows Why Good Scheduling Promotes Better Decisions. *ABA Journal.* Retrieved from abajournal.com

Whittier, J. G. (2000). *The Poetry of John Greenleaf Whittier: A Readers' Edition.* Richmond, Indiana. Friends United Press.

www.ingramcontent.com/pod-product-compliance
Lightning Source LLC
LaVergne TN
LVHW041628070426
835507LV00008B/513